Reflective Writing for Nursing, Health and Social Work

Reflective Writing for Nursing, Health and Social Work

Elizabeth Tanguay, Peter Hanratty and Ben Martin

First published 2020 by
RED GLOBE PRESS

Red Globe Press in the UK is an imprint of Macmillan Education Limited, registered in England, company number 01755588, of 4 Crinan Street, London, N1 9XW.

Red Globe Press® is a registered trademark in the United States, the United Kingdom, Europe and other countries.

ISBN 978-1-352-00996-5 paperback

This book is printed on paper suitable for recycling and made from fully managed and sustained forest sources. Logging, pulping and manufacturing processes are expected to conform to the environmental regulations of the country of origin.

A catalogue record for this book is available from the British Library.

A catalog record for this book is available from the Library of Congress.

Contents

Introduction

Why reflective assignments?

Reflective writing is an integral part of university-level nursing, health and social work programmes but it is a type of writing that students often struggle with. While there are a number of guides on reflective writing, there are few aimed specifically at nursing, health, and social work students. Equally, while there are a number of books on writing for nursing, health, and social work students, none of them deal specifically with reflective writing.

This book focuses specifically on reflective writing for nursing, health, and social work students. It takes you step by step through the process of planning and writing a reflective assignment, dealing with issues relating to content and language. The book is written by three study skills lecturers experienced in helping students to improve their reflective writing. In this book, we draw on what we teach our own students in class as well as our experiences of conducting hundreds of one-to one appointments with students across different disciplines. We have included frequently asked questions as well as examples and exercises to help you develop your reflective academic writing style and avoid common pitfalls.

How to use this book

You can read the advice sections of this book and tips as you are writing and dip into specific chapters, or you can read it cover to cover. However, reflecting and writing are both skills that need to be practiced. We find that students get the most out of the material when they work through the exercises. Part I of the book will get you started on your reflective writing. Here we explain key concepts in reflection, assignment structure, and style as well as the process of writing reflective assignments. Part II covers in detail the most crucial element of truly critical reflective writing – linking theory to practice. This second section will help you develop the level of critical reflection required through undergraduate to postgraduate level and for your continuing professional development.

What is in each chapter?

PART I. Reflective Writing: First Steps

Chapter 1. Types of Reflective Writing
Discover the types of reflective assignment that you might be expected to produce while at university and how you can best prepare for these.

Chapter 2. What Is Reflection and Why Is It Important?
Learn about the process of reflection and why it is so important for nursing, health and social work students.

Chapter 3. The Reflective Writing Journey
Move from the notes you make while on placement to a piece of writing that you can hand in for assessment.

Chapter 4. Capturing Reflections While on Placement
Learn what you should record while on placement and how you can find the time to do this.

Chapter 5. How to Identify Themes
Learn to quickly and easily identify themes from your notes. Understand how to identify the broader themes relating to the literature arising from your experiences and have confidence to write about them. Learn about researching themes from the literature and strategies for making effective notes from the literature.

Chapter 6. Approaching Reflective Writing – Frameworks, Models and Cycles
Explore the different frameworks, models and cycles for reflection, and the benefits and drawbacks of each.

Chapter 7. Planning
Overcome one of the most common barriers to effective writing: planning. The first step to this is planning your time. Then, with the help of a reflective journal and a living plan, you will be able to plan your work so it becomes less of a daunting task.

Chapter 8. The Style of Reflective Academic Writing
Achieve a style of writing that is reflective, allowing you to write about your experiences, while also maintaining an 'academic' style. Learn to switch between the slightly different writing styles you need for each section of your assignment with ease.

Chapter 9. Introductions for Reflective Assignments
Craft effective introductions for different types of reflective writing – learn what to include and how to structure introductions.

Chapter 10. Paragraphs for Reflective Assignments

Create effective and logical paragraphs in your reflective writing.

Chapter 11. Conclusions for Reflective Assignments

Conclude your reflective writing assignment in a way that leaves a strong lasting impression – learn what to include and how to structure conclusions.

PART II. Linking Theory to Practice

Learn one of the most important skills for reflective writing: to write about others' work in a way that links it to your practice. Three crucial techniques for writing about others' work are covered in Chapters 12 and 14.

Chapter 12. Theory to Practice – First Steps

Understand the requirements of linking theory to practice, including how and when to include definitions within your work. Understand the kind of evidence to draw upon and how to order it.

Chapter 13. Incorporating Sources into Your Reflective Writing

Make effective use of quotes, paraphrases and summaries, and understand how to incorporate these within your writing and avoid 'academic misconduct'.

Chapter 14. Writing Critically and Writing with Flow

Find out how to write critically and link themes from the literature to your own experiences in order to show how reflection has led to a growing understanding of your own practice. Learn how to build arguments and avoid being overly descriptive and learn what kind of critical analysis is expected at different stages of your academic journey. Connect ideas in your writing so that the ideas flow logically from beginning to end.

Chapter 15. Editing and Proofreading Your Reflective Assignment

Understand the key differences between editing and proofreading and why it is important to separate these processes. Master techniques to help you edit and proofread your own work and overcome 'blindness' to your own errors.

Chapter 16. Reflective Writing for Professional Development

Continue your reflective practice beyond your university studies and learn some of the key writing skills required for reflective professional development. Develop the skills needed to integrate reflective practice alongside a busy workload.

Appendix 1. Examples of Different Types of Reflective Writing

This appendix gives you a number of extracts from different types of student work, annotated with the features discussed throughout the book to give you a deeper understanding of how you can apply the techniques learned to your own work. The examples are drawn from a number of different nursing, health and social work fields.

Appendix 2. Quick Grammar Guide

This appendix will help you fine-tune your punctuation, one of the key elements of effective academic writing.

Appendix 3. Feedback Glossary

This glossary shows common terms used by lecturers in written feedback. It will help you understand what you need to do to address these comments and signpost you to relevant sections of the book where you can find further guidance.

Answers

Further Reading

PART

1

Reflective Writing: First Steps

CHAPTER

1

Types of Reflective Writing

By the end of this chapter you should:

- Recognise the different types of reflective writing you may be asked to do
- Know what a reflective assignment question looks like and what to include

So what types of reflective writing might you be asked to do at university? You may have already written a reflective piece of coursework and you may realise that reflective writing comes in many forms. The following are some of the most common types of reflective assignment in nursing, health or social work programmes:

Reflective journal

This is probably the first type of reflective writing you will do and indeed you may already be used to writing a reflective journal. You may or may not need to hand in your reflective journal, but the key is to make regular entries and remember to be honest. Your journal is best written in the first person (this means using *I* or *we*), and even if you do hand in extracts of your journal as part of your reflective assignment, these extracts should not read like academic writing.

Some questions to get you started writing journal entries:

What happened? How did I feel at the time? How do I feel now, looking back at the event? What would I do differently next time?

You can prepare for writing a journal by practising writing about your daily experiences and getting used to being honest when you write. Though it may feel uncomfortable at first, the more you do this, the more naturally it will come, and the more easily you will be able to write your journal entries. With journals, it is best to write little and often, as it can be difficult to remember how you felt if you leave it too long after the event.

Reflective essay

A number of different assignments may come under the broad heading of 'essay' and sometimes the word essay is used to describe any extended piece of writing you may be asked to do. Often you will be given a particular topic or *theme* to write about, around which you base your reflection. For example, you may be asked to discuss the theme of dignity through reflecting on different elements of your own practice. In this case, you will need to ensure that the examples that you think of can be easily connected to the theme that you are being asked to discuss.

An example of a reflective essay question might be:

With reference to your own experience in practice, reflect on your understanding of the importance of maintaining dignity as a mental health nurse.

To answer this question, you might like to think of three sub themes under the heading of dignity (for example, privacy, communication and autonomy) and relate each of these themes to examples from your own experiences.

To prepare for writing this type of assignment, make sure you keep notes while on placement. You may like to leave a margin to jot down themes that occur to you at the time or when you read back over your notes; or, if you already know possible themes you will be writing about, you can 'collect' your thoughts under different themed headings and start to read more about these themes.

Patchwork assignment or patchwork essay

A patchwork assignment requires you to reflect on a number of different artefacts that you choose or produce yourself, including, for example, journal entries, pictures or poems. This is a relatively new type of assignment, developed, among other reasons, in order to combat the problem of students leaving assignments to the last minute. The idea is that while a patchwork essay is an integrated piece of work, you complete short segments of writing over the course of a module to avoid the panic of having to finish a whole essay. (Of course, we know the reality is often different and you may still be faced with having to finish the assignment in one go!) Even if a patchwork assignment is an unfamiliar format for you, if you remember the different elements of reflection that need to be included and devise a clear structure for your assignment, it isn't any more difficult than other types of reflective assignment.

An example question for a patchwork assignment might be:

Use three patches to illustrate and analyse your professional and personal development during the second year of your degree.

In this example, possible patches might be a journal entry where you reflect on how you have developed your ability to communicate with clients. You might include a picture of a snowy mountain which you link to some aspect of practice which you thought was insurmountable or particularly daunting but that you managed to conquer. Another patch could be based around a map in which you write about how you tried to navigate your way through a tricky situation and the resources you drew on.

To help prepare for patchwork assignments, try recording your journal entries in different formats; for example, through writing a short poem about your experiences or drawing pictures. Also look out for interesting artefacts you might see when you are out and about that you could reflect on. For example, a picture on a café wall or some text on a postcard could provide some inspiration.

Reflection on an incident

You may be asked to choose a particular incident that happened while on placement and to reflect on it while not being given any broad theme. In this case you will need to decide on a theme or themes emerging from the experience that you want to explore further and any related sub-themes (for example, advocacy in nursing might be your overall theme and your subthemes may be decision-making, communication, and autonomy). You would need to ensure that the incident that you choose has enough examples of situations for each of these subthemes.

An example essay question for reflecting on an incident might be:

Reflect on an encounter with a service user.

To prepare for writing this type of assignment, make sure you keep notes while on practice of any potential or noteworthy 'incidents'. You may like to leave a margin to jot down themes that occur to you at the time or when you read back over your notes.

Reflection on a placement

This is similar to the assignment of reflecting on an incident, in that it is up to you to decide which themes to discuss. In this case, however, you might include examples from a number of different incidents rather than from one incident. Again, make sure the incidents you choose from the placement tie in to the overall themes you have chosen. If you do reflect on a number of incidents you should ensure your reflection does not become too superficial. It is far better to focus on a small number of events and reflect in detail on these.

An example essay question for reflecting on a placement might be:

Reflect on your experience working as a paramedic.

Again, to prepare for writing this type of assignment, make sure you keep notes while on placement of any potential or noteworthy 'incidents'. You may like to leave a margin to jot down themes that occur to you at the time or when you read back over your notes.

Other types of reflective assignment

While we have given you some indication of possible reflective assignments, there may be other forms of reflective writing that you need to submit. Reflection may be part or all of an assignment.

Types of reflection for higher degrees, research degrees and for CPD

While we start with the very basics of reflection in this book, the types, structure and basic components of reflective writing will be similar at different levels. What will differ is the level of critical analysis you will need to include. The increasing level of criticality you will need as you progress through your studies and career is addressed in Chapters 14 and 16.

Summary

- Different types of assignment come under the bracket of reflective writing
- Find out the type of assignment you are expected to write and what format it will take
- Capture your thoughts in a reflective journal, and link key themes together. This will give you a firm foundation for your assignments

CHAPTER

2

What Is Reflection and Why Is It Important?

By the end of this chapter you should:

- Understand reflection and reflective practice
- Know the benefits of reflection and reflective practice
- Recognise the purpose and aims of reflective writing in a university and/or a professional context
- Realise the benefits of keeping a reflective journal
- Understand the three main elements of reflection

Reflective writing is an important element of nursing, health and social work courses, but what is reflection and why do we do it? This chapter will help you understand what reflection and reflective practice are, why your lecturers want you to write reflectively, and the benefits that such writing can bring to your academic and continuing professional development.

What is reflection?

Consider this simple example of reflection:

> A few years ago, my husband and I were on our way to a wedding in the little town in Italy that I had worked in as a new teacher a few years earlier. I couldn't wait to revisit places I had known and to catch up with old friends. All our bags were packed, I had checked and double-checked that we had our passports, wallets and tickets as well as our insurance details. We left four hours earlier than needed to make sure we'd get to the airport in time, only to realise that our flight was actually booked for a day later. We decided to stay overnight in the airport lounge rather than trying to book a hotel as we were both skint postgraduate students at the time. The lounge was noisy all through the night and the lights remained on, which meant that we didn't get much sleep. Despite

being grumpy the next morning, we were ready in plenty of time for our flight and flew without any problems to our destination where we had a fantastic time at the wedding catching up with old friends, followed by a great week afterwards eating delicious local seafood and snorkelling in clear blue waters.

Returning from holiday and recounting the trip to others, the fact that we were a day early for the flight was something to laugh about – at least it was better than being a day late! However, I thought, if only I had double-checked the date on the booking, we wouldn't have had to sleep overnight in the airport lounge and arrive tired and ratty at the other end. I decided the reason we were so early and so well prepared is probably because I am the kind of person who hates being late for anything. On the upside, we had a fantastic time seeing old friends, and stayed in a lovely apartment. The food had been fabulous as it's fresh and plentiful at that time of year in the area. All in all, it was a great holiday, and we'll certainly go back, but I decided that next time I'll be sure to write reminders on my phone calendar and my physical calendar and to double check the date on the booking at least a week before we leave. I will also ask my husband not to presume that I have taken care of everything and to double check all the dates and times himself!

This anecdote exemplifies the informal reflection we might do in our everyday lives. In the example, the author considers what happened, what was positive or negative about this, along with *why* it happened in the way it did and what she might learn from the situation. Put simply, reflection is an exercise in learning from your experiences so that you can do better next time. Reflection doesn't only have to draw from negative experiences (like arriving on the wrong date at the airport), though this is the most common type of reflection we might naturally do. After all, it is human nature to dwell on the negatives. Positive experiences can also be learned from (the seafood was delicious; we'll certainly order that again, and the apartment was great, so that's somewhere I'd like to return).

Reflective practice expands the value that we may gain from reflection in our everyday lives and uses it in the context of professional practice, or, in the case of university assignments, during our *training* for professional practice. Reflection helps us to move from novice to expert in our profession. Christopher Johns, one of the key experts on reflective practice in healthcare, recognises that though we may learn from subconscious reflection, deliberate reflection can speed up the transition from novice to expert (Johns, 2017). He notes too, how reflective practice is on a continuum from 'from *doing reflection* to *being reflective*' and 'from a technical rational to a professional artistry perspective'

(Johns, 2017, p. 6). This means that through engaging in deliberate reflection, we learn to become increasingly critical, or analytical, examining what we are doing and why, rather than merely 'going through the motions'. Eventually, reflection will become less about the technicalities of 'doing reflection' and more about *being* a reflective practitioner.

The reflective process is cyclical – that is, it is ongoing. You will learn from your experiences and, as a result, decide to act in a certain way in the future. Following that, you will reflect on the new experiences, and so the cycle continues. In terms of reflecting on your role in nursing, health or social work, reflection is not only something that you will do while you are a student. You will hear terms like *reflection-in-action* and *reflection-on-action* (Schön, 1983). For now, all you need to remember is that *reflection-in-action* is the reflection you do while you are experiencing the event (it is more than merely thinking about the event while it is happening, but can also involve 'reframing' the event by viewing it from a different perspective). *Reflection-on-action* is thinking about an experience afterwards. Reflection-in-action is the type of reflection that you will commonly do once you have gained a wealth of experience and this reflection will eventually come naturally. In the meantime (and afterwards as well), a systematic process of reflection-on-action can help you to become a more experienced and confident practitioner. The writing you do for your university assignments will largely reflect *on* action.

Why are you asked to write reflectively?

As with any writing, the first thing to do is understand your audience and what they want from you. If you remember the three main reasons you are being asked to write reflectively, this will help considerably. These three main reasons for writing reflectively at university are to show that you can:

1 Look back and learn from your experiences
2 Through reference to academic literature, understand possible reasons for your experiences and how your actions demonstrate evidence-based practice
3 Understand the reflective process and present ideas logically

If you keep these three reasons in mind throughout the planning and writing process, you will make sure you tick all the boxes for that piece of reflective coursework. Let's look at these three reasons in more detail.

1 You can learn from your experiences

The first skill your lecturers want you to demonstrate is that you can look back and learn from your experiences, whether positive or negative.

Don't forget to mention what went well and what you can learn from this. Effective reflection can lead to change in a positive way but doesn't always need to be based on negative experiences. Think about why your experiences went so well and draw confidence from this for the future. Equally, don't be afraid of writing about the negative experiences as often these provide a rich source for reflection.

2 You understand how your experiences relate to the wider academic context and demonstrate evidence-based practice

The second skill that your lecturers want you to demonstrate is that you are able to relate your experiences to themes in the relevant academic literature and use this literature to help deepen your understanding of your own experiences. Your experience will not be unique to you. Others will have experienced similar things before you and will do so after you. Academics will have written about such experiences and thought about why they happen, or the best way to go about something. Why does something make you feel a particular way? Why should something be done in a certain way? Relating your own experiences to the wider academic context is the most analytical and critical aspect of the writing and where you have the opportunity to gain the most marks for your assignments. (See Chapters 12 through 14 for more on this.)

3 You can present your ideas clearly and structure your writing logically

The final major aspect of your writing that your lecturers will want to see is that you understand the reflective process and, as with any academic writing, that you can structure your writing logically. You will need to think about the reflective framework, model or cycle that you are using, how to structure your assignment in terms of the different sections that you need to include, and how to make your writing 'flow' through connecting sections, paragraphs and sentences into a cohesive piece of work.

The benefits of reflective practice

Aside from passing your university course, there are other benefits to engaging in the reflective process.

Being reflective can help you to:

- Become a better practitioner as you look back on what worked and what didn't work and why, and 'bank' these reflections in your growing evidence base to improve your future practice.

- Become more self-aware and more confident in your own practice as you learn that there are areas you can succeed in already, that mistakes are crucial to self-improvement and how to deal with negative experiences and move on.
- Show your employers that you can learn from your experiences and build on your practice – a crucial element for career progression in many nursing, health or social work fields and often mandatory for revalidation.

When you are highly stressed or under increasing pressure at work, it can be tempting to think that you have not got time for reflective practice. However, reflection may be one of the things that can help you keep going when times are tough. Reflection can help you learn from your own experiences as well as from experiences others have documented in the literature. It can be hugely comforting to realise that others have faced the same difficulties as you. The skills you are learning now as a student will benefit you far beyond your university course. So, try and get into the practice of developing good reflective practice now.

The three elements of reflection

The three basic components of the reflective process are *Experience, Reflection* and *Action.* This is known as the ERA model of reflection (Bassot, 2016). For your university assignments you need to:

1 Describe the events
2 Think about what was positive or negative about the events, consider *why* they happened, and relate these to broader themes in the literature
3 Think about how what you learned from the events can influence your practice going forward

In the previous example, though a much simpler example than you will be working with, the three ERA components are:

1 Experience – packing bags, arriving at the airport early, spending a night in the airport hotel and arriving in time for the wedding.
2 Reflection – The positive elements were being prepared and enjoying the food and location; the negative part was having to spend a night sleeping in the airport and being grumpy the next day as a result. I thought that the

reason this had probably happened was because I always like to be early for everything and had been so focussed on this that I hadn't double-checked the date. I also thought that perhaps my husband would have checked the dates and he thought that I would have.

3 Action – What I know now is that next time I go on holiday, I will send the dates to my phone, set a reminder the week before and double-check the dates and times.

When recounting an anecdote about a less than successful experience, the different parts of the reflection might appear in any order. However, lecturers like writing that is logical and structured. To help with this structure, there are a number of different approaches to reflection (called frameworks, models or cycles) which all more or less cover the different aspects of reflection we have noted. For now, just remember these question prompts for the three components as noted by Driscoll (2007):

- **Experience: What?**
- **Reflection: So what?**
- **Action: Now what?**

What?

What exactly happened?

So what?

What was positive or negative about this?
Why did this happen?

Now what?

As a result of your reflection, what will you do next time? (adapted from Driscoll, 2007).

So, the three elements of reflective process are the 'thing' or event you are reflecting on, the reflection itself and the action that you take from this to change your behaviour in the future.

As noted, the process is cyclical, so could be represented as follows (Figure 2.1).

Now it's time to try a basic exercise in reflection.

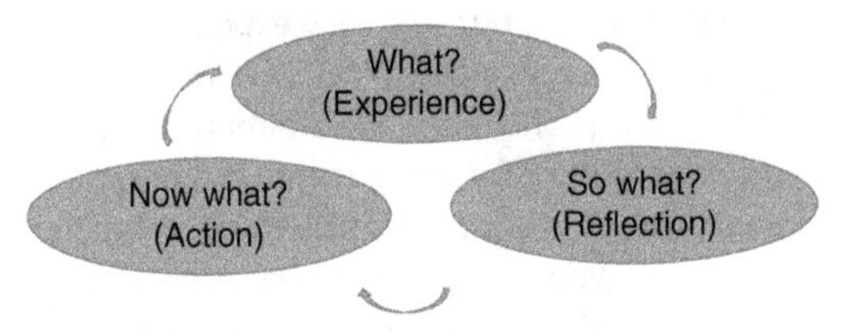

Figure 2.1 The reflective process cycle (inspired by Bassot, 2016)

EXERCISE 2.1

Think back to the first day or week of your studies and add notes under the headings in the box. Perhaps you couldn't find the room for a certain course, perhaps you found a particular talk very useful or didn't understand much of what was going on. Why did these things happen in the way that they did? What past experiences helped you to understand what happened? Perhaps you have realised you need to do some more background reading on a particular area of studies in order to follow what the lecturers are saying. Perhaps it is a long time since you studied and after a session with a librarian, you realise you need to look into using referencing software. If you haven't yet started studying, think about another significant event (a holiday/a disagreement with a family member or acquaintance/a party you organised).

What happened? Experience

List the different things that you did in the week

So what? Reflection

What went well? What didn't go well? Why was this?

Now what? Action

What have you learned that you can use in the future? What action will you take as a result?

Sitting down to think about our everyday experiences is not something we do regularly, as many of the things that we do are automatic (for example, making a cup of coffee). We are more likely to reflect on events that are momentous, or for some reason didn't go as well as we might have hoped (such as missing a flight). Some of the things you may have done as you started your course might have been new or unfamiliar to you, and some of the other events you may have chosen to reflect on for Exercise 2.1 are also out of the ordinary. Of course, all these events are simplified, and not related to any academic sources (how to link your experiences to the academic literature is explored in Part II of this book). However, if you remember these three crucial elements of reflection that you thought about while doing the reflection task, you will be on the right track.

Summary

- Reflective practice as expressed through reflective writing is an integral part of nursing, health or social work programmes at university
- The benefits of reflection will help you beyond your course
- The three main elements of reflection answer the questions 'What?', 'So what?' and 'Now what?'
- Your lecturers are looking to see that you can (1) learn from your experiences, (2) link practice to theory and (3) write logically

CHAPTER

3

The Reflective Writing Journey

By the end of this chapter you should:

- Understand the steps in the reflective writing journey
- Know what your end goal is and how to get there

This is a book about reflective *writing,* and for us, writing is a key element of the reflective process. The reflective process includes writing throughout. It is not just a case of thinking and *then* writing up your assignment. Writing at each stage of the process, when you are planning, as well as when you are recording your emotions can help to clarify your thoughts. This chapter covers the main steps to your reflective writing journey.

Planning your time

Before writing a reflective assignment, as with any project, it's a good idea to have some plan of action. You need to know what your goal for reflection is (what type of writing are you going to need to produce? what is your assignment question? and how long have you got?). All of the other steps can fit into this plan.

Capturing reflections while on placement

Your plan should give you some idea of how you are going to capture notes while you are on placement. Be specific about this. When will you write? Where will you write? When you are at work or at home, digitally or in a journal?

Identifying themes in your notes

To write your assignments, you'll need to draw out themes from your notes. You can start identifying these themes while you are writing your notes as well and highlight events that you think may fit into a particular theme that you know you will want to write about or that you have covered in your lectures or your reading.

Reading for themes

Once you have identified the themes you are going to write about, you'll need to read up more on these in journal articles and textbooks. You'll also need to start developing an effective system for taking notes and recording your sources if you don't already have one.

Writing your reflective assignment

Having planned your time wisely and made notes of events and kept records of your reading, you'll be in a great position to write your assignment. Now you need to plan a structure for your assignment, work out what you are going to include, and what you will include in each section.

Writing with style

When writing up your assignment, more than when you were keeping notes on placement, you need to think about the style of your writing.

Editing and proofreading

Once you've written your assignment, you can edit for style and content, proofread for any obvious errors, and check your referencing.

Summary

- Think of the reflection process as a journey
- You will need a plan for your journey
- Writing is not the end point of the journey but takes place throughout

CHAPTER

4

Capturing Reflections While on Placement

By the end of this chapter, you should:

- Understand the benefits of keeping a reflective journal
- Know *what* to write about, *when* to write, and *how* to write

The benefits of keeping a reflective journal

Even if you don't need to include any elements of your journal within your reflective assignment, it is a good idea to keep a journal when you are on placement. In your journal, you can include your descriptions of the events and how you felt about them at the time as well as anything else that occurs to you. You probably won't use the journal word for word when you come to write up your assignments, but it will make it a lot easier to select events to write about and to remember how you were feeling at the time. You may even find that you enjoy keeping a journal for your own growth. It can help you to work things out and it can be fascinating to look back and see how you have grown in confidence from even a few months ago as your experience increases.

What to include in your reflective journal

You can keep the loose ERA (Experience, Reflection, Action – see Chapter 2) structure in your mind to help you when you are writing your journal. You'll want to include descriptions of events that may have seemed significant to you at the time or made you feel a certain way. Try to write about positive as well as negative events. A detailed description of an event may be useful, along with any information you know you will be asked for in your assignment. You might jot down some ideas about why the event happened and, if it occurs to you, a note about the literature. For example, 'check the article Dr. Smith mentioned in the lecture last week'.

Table 4.1 provides a suggested format for keeping a journal that can make the task seem less daunting, but still lends itself to easy transfer to reflective assignments with the ERA elements. Making notes on positive as well as negative aspects of your experiences will mean you don't only reflect on what went wrong.

Table 4.1 Suggested format for journal entries

	Comments (reasons/themes etc.)
One good thing that happened today *The new mother said she would stop giving the baby juice from a bottle after I talked through the leaflets on weaning.*	– *Importance of health education* – *Role of the health visitor* – *Nutrition and babies*
How I felt *I felt so nervous when I realised I would need to intervene and scared of saying anything.*	*Nervous as I was younger than the mother* *Thought she might think I was interfering.*
How I feel now *Proud that I helped* *Relieved I did say something even though I was scared* *Eager to go to see the mother at the next visit and see how she is getting on* *Excited about the next challenge.*	*Confidence – grows with experience* *Important to do what I know is right even if uncomfortable* *I know I can do it!!!!*
One bad thing that happened today *I could see that the young mother was upset when I asked how she was feeling but wasn't sure what to say or how to help.*	*Postnatal depression – peaks at which month? Check journal article from lecture again.*
How I felt – *Clumsy* – *Stupid – didn't know what to say* – *Sad that I couldn't help* – *Worried about leaving her*	*Communication* *Read up on helping new mothers with PND.*
How I feel now *Sorry that I didn't think of referring her for an appointment with the GP or recommending baby groups but glad that Sally stepped in to do this.*	*Find out about baby groups and support networks in the area.*

EXERCISE 4.1

You might find it best to try this exercise once you are on placement before you start writing your journal. Use the template to write about your day. Once you have done this, experiment with different formats.

	Comments (reasons/themes etc.)
One good thing that happened today	
How I felt	
How I feel now	
One bad thing that happened today	
How I felt	
How I feel now	

When to write

When you are on placement, finding the time to write a journal as well as completing your assignments can seem impossible. But you don't need to find huge chunks of time. We find our students write more in their journals and find the writing more useful if they write little and often. Writing in your journal regularly will save you a lot of time and stress when you come to write up your assignment. If you make journal writing a habit rather than a chore you only do occasionally, you may surprise yourself and actually enjoy the process!

If you prioritise writing in your day by timetabling it, you will make sure that these writing sessions are more likely to happen. For example, at the end of a working week, look at your calendar and block off five 10-minute slots for writing in the next week and then stick to them. If you miss a writing session, then make up for it. After all, you only need to find 10 minutes.

When you timetable your writing, don't wait until you have a large 'chunk' of time – often this just isn't realistic. It's far better to do 'little and often' sessions, than to wait for that magical day of writing that may never materialise (then if that chunk of time does arrive, you'll find you have done a lot of the thinking beforehand and just need to pull it all together).

Choose a time of day that suits you best. If you find it easier to write in the morning, then set your alarm 10 minutes earlier rather than forcing yourself to write at the end of a busy evening shift. Or, if you are working nights, you might write before you start your night shift. Thinking carefully about how you use your time in advance means you won't waste your best time of day scrolling through social media.

EXERCISE 4.2

In the box, plan three writing sessions for the week ahead. First, write down your existing commitments such as placement times, lectures and any other activities that are organised for the week. Then, identify three times where you can fit in short writing sessions. If you haven't started placement yet and want to try the exercise, that's fine. You can use these sessions to reflect on elements of your course that are going well or badly. The aim is to establish a journaling habit and see how writing can fit into your life.

Day	Plans for the day and writing times (if any)
Monday	
Tuesday	
Wednesday	
Thursday	
Friday	
Saturday	
Sunday	

How to write

In your reflective journal, you don't need to worry about the style of what you are writing. Be spontaneous in your reflection. It may be that you need to reword your reflection afterwards to make it part of your assignment, but the more you allow yourself to be 'free' in your reflection, the more useful it will be.

You can jot things down in bullet points, full sentences, shorthand or in another language if you prefer. Have a look back at the extract from the student health visitor's journal on p. 22. The student has used a mix of full sentences, notes and bullet points. Write however you need to in order to keep yourself writing about your experiences. These are really notes for you rather than anyone else, but try and make them easy to read and access when you're referring to them to write your assignment.

Try experimenting with different ways of recording your reflections. You can be as creative as you like and make your journal visually interesting through use of mindmaps, pictures and colour. If you are a techie, use your phone or tablet to make notes or dictate your thoughts; if you prefer stationery, invest in a wonderful bound notebook that you will enjoy writing in!

Summary

- Journaling will make it easier to write your assignments
- Habitual reflection will help you with your professional development
- Write about what happened and how you felt and leave space for the 'Why?' questions
- Journal in whatever way you feel most comfortable – write bullet points, full sentences or use pictures
- Experiment using a notebook, keeping an electronic journal or try dictating your thoughts and recording them on your phone

CHAPTER

5

How to Identify Themes

By the end of this chapter, you should be able to:

- Understand what a theme is and use techniques to help identify themes from your work
- Understand the importance of themes in your reflection
- Recognise how themes help analysis of your reflection
- Organise themes logically

What is a theme?

A theme is an area which you can base your research and reflection around. Think of the kinds of keywords you would search a library catalogue or the internet for if you wanted information. For example, 'communication', 'privacy' or 'consent'. Once you have a journal full of notes, it's time to start looking at these for common themes. By correctly identifying the themes for your reflection, you will be able to focus your research better and improve your practice.

Identifying themes is an aspect of reflective writing which can cause some difficulties for students. This is because the material presented in our reflective accounts is usually written in reference to a specific event or events which have been encountered in the past. Being able to fit this event around a broad theme (such as 'communication', 'privacy' or 'consent') is not always an obvious link to make but it is a necessary step in being able to reflect in an analytical way and identify aspects of practice which are strengths and those which are opportunities for improvement.

This chapter is divided into four key principles for identifying themes:

1. Organising and annotating your material
2. Thinking broadly
3. Naming your themes
4. Presenting themes logically

Organising and annotating your material

A common problem in thematic analysis stems from the logical arrangement of ideas, and is often a result of writers not following an organised process when handling their material.

Consider the following extract from an Osteopathy student's reflective journal:

> 10.05 am – Mr Williams hobbles in to the consultation room. He is making loud noises as he walks and plonks himself down heavily in the chair. He is breathing very heavily and appears visibly agitated and gives very short, snappy yes or no answers to my initial small talk.
>
> He ranks himself 10 on the pain score chart – says that he hasn't slept a wink for weeks and that his lower back is the reason for this. He asks for a glass of water midway through the case history so I go out to the lobby to get him one. When I return, we continue the consultation. As I continue to build a history of this condition, Mr Williams seems to get more and more agitated. He asks me to stop talking so loudly and get on with it. His foot is tapping the floor quickly and he keeps looking out of the window. As I progress through the consultation, I notice his behaviour and ask him if he is comfortable. After a few seconds, Mr Williams apologises and says that he is feeling anxious and has been struggling with a low mood.

As a journal entry, this is written chronologically. That is natural and perfectly fine for a journal. However, it doesn't lend itself to the easy identification of themes.

Writing notes can help to make sense of your reflection and represents an important stage of the process of material organisation. The first step in organising your material is to make a copy of your reflective journal/description of the scenario. The purpose of making a copy is so that you can make notes on the copy; trying to make notes on the original copy can sometimes result in a difficult-to-read description. Once you have copied your description, make **notes relating to what happened** in the margins (or on your word processor). **These notes should be brief**: avoid the temptation to write full sentences, or to try to identify themes and instead try to identify **key events** in your description.

TIP

Do not try to identify themes at this stage

By allowing yourself to follow a process, you can reduce the risk of misidentifying themes.

Now, before you continue, read the passage again and make notes relating to what happened. As a starting point for making notes, consider these questions:

- How does the entry relate to what you have been studying in lectures?
- Did anything unusual happen?
- What are the 'key' words in the entry?

Thinking broadly

The next step is to collate your notes into broader categories and this is a process which many students find easier to do if they utilise some 'out of the box' techniques.

Agitated

Heavy breathing

10.05 am – Mr Williams hobbles in to the consultation room. He is making loud noises as he walks and plonks himself down heavily in the chair. He is breathing very heavily and appears visibly agitated and gives very short, snappy yes or no answers to my initial small talk.

High ranking

Short answers to yes/no questions

He ranks himself a 10 on the pain score chart– says that he hasn't slept a wink for weeks and that his lower back is the reason for this. He asks for a glass of water midway through the case history so I went out to the lobby to get him one. When I return, we continue the consultation. As I continue to build a history of this condition, Mr Williams seems to get more and more agitated. He asks me to stop talking so loudly and get on with it. His foot is tapping the floor quickly and he keeps looking out of the window. As I progress through the consultation, I notice his behaviour and ask him if he is comfortable. After a few seconds, Mr Williams apologises and says that he is feeling anxious and has been struggling with a low mood.

Anxiety/ low mood

Notice behaviour

Assuming that this passage is representative of the rest of this student's notes, it is easy to see how confusing trying to arrange these could become.

To overcome this, the student could try the following:

- Copy their notes onto paper
- Cut with scissors

If these were your notes, you could cut the paper into bits, and try stacking them in different piles according to similarities. You should try to do this a couple of times and the pace at which you do this should at first be as though you are playing the card game 'Snap'. Try to resist the urge to overthink here and aim for between three and five piles. From this example, everything to do with 'how the patient and I talked' could be put in them same pile and 'how the patient felt' could be put in another.

Name the piles and colour code them

Now that you have piles of similar things, you are ready to 'name' them. These names will be the themes which you have identified from your reflection and will make organisation of your reading and writing much easier.

Table 5.1 shows how a student could have arranged the piled-up notes.

The next question to consider is why these notes have been grouped. What is the common factor between them? Building on the piles of notes relating to 'how the patient and I talked' and 'how the patient felt' allows the student to group the notes into two categories: communication and additional symptoms. The fact that Mr Williams became agitated with the volume and pace of questions, that he gave short answers to questions which could be answered yes or no, and that the student noticed his behaviour and responded to it are related to communication. On the other hand, the high pain score, Mr Williams' anxiety, low mood and his heavy breathing could all relate to additional symptoms related with low back pain.

It makes sense at this point to consider how our thoughts and actions so far can help us to organise our reading. It is very important to develop

Table 5.1 The arrangement of notes

Communication	Additional symptoms
Agitated with volume and pace	High pain score
Short answers to yes/no questions	Anxiety
Notice behaviour	Low mood
	Heavy breathing

active approaches to reading (see Chapter 12), and one of the ways which you can do this is by colour coding the themes you have identified here. Let's imagine that you have these two themes: A: Communication and B: Additional Symptoms. To make your life easier, assign a highlighter colour to each theme: Communication = yellow and Additional Symptoms = green.

Now when you are reading literature pick up a highlighter with a purpose. For example, if you pick up a green highlighter, look for information which is relevant only to your second theme (here: additional symptoms of low back pain). If you prefer to use a computer to read, consider how creating folders can help you to organise reading materials by theme – for example, you could name folders according to your identified themes and arrange literature by these folders as in Figure 5.1.

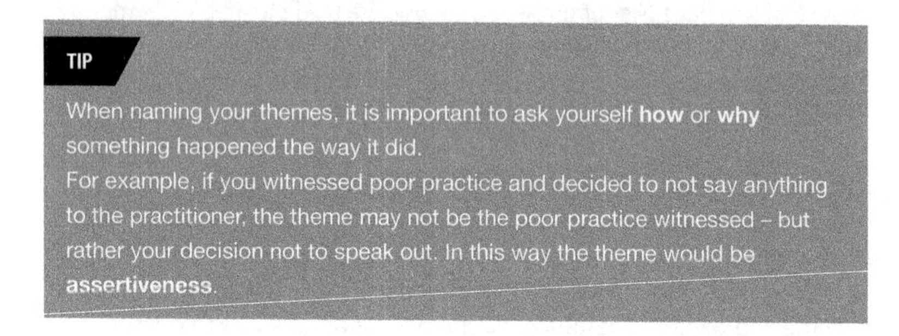

TIP

When naming your themes, it is important to ask yourself **how** or **why** something happened the way it did.

For example, if you witnessed poor practice and decided to not say anything to the practitioner, the theme may not be the poor practice witnessed – but rather your decision not to speak out. In this way the theme would be **assertiveness**.

Another way that you can make use of computers to help you with identifying themes is to use a spreadsheet to arrange information. There are many ways to do this, but you could try making titles along the top row of a spreadsheet, as in Figure 5.2 (author, year, title, conclusion, etc.).

The titles you decide to give each column in your spreadsheet will be up to you, but a good starting point would be to think about including the necessary bibliographic information (author's name, year, title, etc.) You could also include columns such as conclusions, methodologies, and

Figure 5.1 Create folders to help organise your work

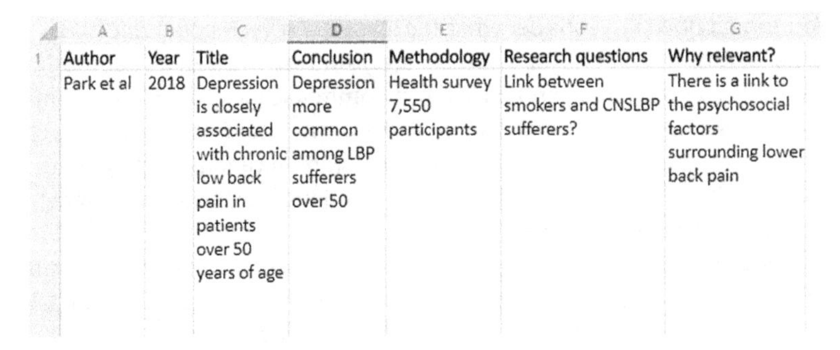

	A	B	C	D	E	F	G
1	Author	Year	Title	Conclusion	Methodology	Research questions	Why relevant?
	Park et al	2018	Depression is closely associated with chronic low back pain in patients over 50 years of age	Depression more common among LBP sufferers over 50	Health survey 7,550 participants	Link between smokers and CNSLBP sufferers?	There is a iink to the psychosocial factors surrounding lower back pain

Figure 5.2 Use a spreadsheet to help arrange your research

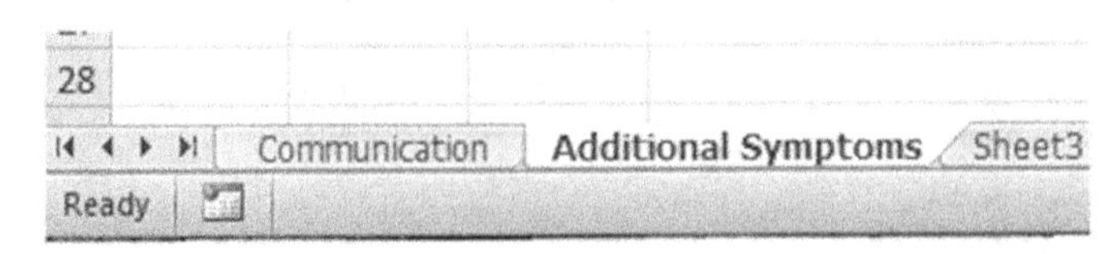

Figure 5.3 You can name the different sheets according to your themes

research questions. Naming each of these columns can encourage you to look for specific pieces of information in your reading material – and this makes the task of reading much easier.

If you decide to try the spreadsheet method – consider having different sheets to represent the themes you have identified, as shown in Figure 5.3.

These are some of the ways which can help you to makes sense of themes. It is a good idea to try them all to see which works best for you.

Presenting themes logically

Your themes will now be derived from the experience(s) which you have selected for reflection. You will now have highlighted different academic texts which relate to your identified themes. The next step is to consider how these highlighted sections should be best presented in your assignment. Which theme should come first? Why? Could you apply a chronological order by presenting the themes in the order in which they happened during the event? Is there a different procedural order? Is one theme more important than the others, or do you have more to write about it?

You should now also consider what the literature reveals about effective patient communication. For example, are yes/no answers always appropriate? How can volume and pace affect communication? How important is body language to communication, and are there common behaviours which practitioners can identify? How can communication affect patient outcomes? Are there obligations which practitioners are required to meet in regards to communication?

Consider the following extracts and how you could use information from them to help support and explore the themes identified in 5.1 (see Assignment 2 in Appendix 1 for how these have been integrated) (Figure 5.4).

STANDARD OF PROFICIENCY	
STANDARDS	**GUIDANCE**
A1 You must have well-developed interpersonal communication skills and the ability to adapt communication strategies to suit the specific needs of a patient.	1. Your skills should include an ability to: 1.1. Be sensitive to the range and forms of communication. 1.2. Select effective forms of communication. 1.3. Move between different forms of communication for individual patients. Note also: A2-A6

Figure 5.4 General Osteopathic Council's Osteopathic Practice Standards, 2012

Chronic pain is a major health problem and has high comorbidity with depression (35%) and other psychological problems. The cognitive-behavioural perspective introduced in 1983 emphasized the role of attributions, efficacy expectations, personal control, and problem solving. Cognitive behavioural therapy (CBT) became the standard treatment for chronic pain patients who have to deal with psychological distress and disabilities. CBT incorporates both cognitive (for example, cognitive restructuring) and behavioural techniques (operant or respondent learning) to alter behaviour. Although there is sound evidence that CBT-based treatments are effective with many disorders, only moderate effect sizes were reported for patients with chronic pain. Moreover, a proportion of patients appear not to benefit from CBT. Therefore, clinicians and researchers have been looking at alternatives.

Summary

- Themes will help you organise your writing and make sense of your reflection
- Think broadly at first
- Make notes from your reflective account
- Use colours, folders and/or spreadsheets to help group things

CHAPTER

6

Approaching Reflective Writing – Frameworks, Models and Cycles

By the end of this chapter you should:

- Understand some different approaches to reflection
- Recognise when each approach is most appropriate
- Know how to describe the advantages of each approach
- Be able to structure your writing according to a particular approach

A number of approaches to reflection have been developed by academics and practitioners in the nursing, health or social work fields. The terms used for these approaches vary from framework to model or cycle. But whatever the name, all the approaches are basically a means of helping to guide your reflection and give structure to your writing. Using a framework, model or cycle will help you plan your work and make writing easier. Using one of these recognised approaches to reflection will help you structure your thoughts and break down your experience to ensure you include what your lecturers are expecting to read in your assignment.

In this chapter we'll think about how each approach can benefit you and work out which is/are best for the piece of reflective writing you are working on. The three approaches we focus on are:

1. A *What? So what?, Now what?* approach (Borton, 1970; Driscoll, 2007; Rolfe, Freshwater and Jasper, 2001)
2. Gibbs' Reflective Cycle (Gibbs, 1988)
3. Kolb's Experiential Learning Cycle (Kolb, 1984)

Even if you have been asked to use a different approach, working through the exercises in this chapter and mapping experiences and reflections to the different approaches presented here will help you when you come to use whichever approach/es you finally decide on.

To provide a clear overview, the approaches are summarised rather than discussed in great detail. For more in-depth treatment of each approach, you can refer to the literature listed in the further reading section at the end of the book.

Select the right approach to reflection

You may have been told which approach to use (check your coursework guidelines carefully to see whether this is the case), or you may need to select one yourself. In either case, you will almost certainly need to give some reasons why you chose to use a particular framework, model, cycle or combination. To help with this, we consider the benefits of using each approach and give you an example scenario from a student's assignment to work with. But remember, even though the approaches present things in different ways, they are all used to aid the common elements of reflection, so you will be expected to include similar information each time. It makes it clearer for your reader if you specify which approach you are using at the start of your assignment.

1 What? So what? Now what? Driscoll (2007)

The approaches in this section all follow a *what? so what? now what?* structure. First used in an educational setting (Borton, 1970), the structure was later applied to clinical supervision (Driscoll, 2007) and nursing settings (Rolfe et al., 2001). We've started with the *What?* approaches because of their simplicity, and because the three basic question prompts are easy to remember. To some extent, the answers to the *What?, So what?,* and *Now what?* questions form the basis of all approaches to reflection and can be seen as equivalents to the event/reflection/action elements in the ERA model discussed in Chapter 2.

Driscoll, in his original model for structured reflection (1994), aimed to offer a practical approach for those new to reflection. He provides a comprehensive list of 'trigger' questions for reflection, and emphasises **the importance of the action that needs to be taken as a result of the reflection** (Driscoll, 2007). Rolfe et al. also developed their model for reflexive practice using the three *What?, So what?,* and *Now what?* questions but repeat the questions at three levels, becoming gradually deeper in reflection. As the name suggests, working through the framework should aid in the development of practice, and the use of *reflexive* in Rolfe et al.'s version places an emphasis on **changing the experience or situation.** Through the remainder of this section, we focus on Driscoll's (2007) model for structured reflection.

Answering the What?, So what?, and Now what? questions

The following questions are adapted from the trigger questions by Driscoll (2007). You don't need to answer all the questions about each situation – just include what is relevant.

What? (The description part)

Answering the following questions will ensure you include everything you need to in your description of the event:

- What is the purpose of returning to this event?
- What happened?
- What did I see and do?
- What was my reaction to it?
- Who else was involved?
- What did these other people do?

Remember, you don't need to write about everything that happened on a particular occasion, just the most significant moments and the parts that you will refer to again in the next sections.

So what? (feelings/evaluation and theory)

This is where you think about the 'meaning' behind what happened. In this section you include your feelings as well as evaluations to write about the positive and negative aspects of events. It is also the most natural place to refer to the broader literature and introduce references to explore key themes, as well as adding any comments that a mentor or supervisor helping you to reflect might have to say.

Ask yourself:

- What worked or didn't work about the experience?
- How did I feel at the time?
- Were my feelings different from those of other people involved at the time? (Of course, you can't 'know' this, unless you ask those people, but you can see how people react.)
- Are my feelings now, after the event, different from those feelings I experienced at the time?
- Do I still feel 'troubled'? If so, in what way? Note that this question assumes that you are reflecting on a negative event. This doesn't need to be the case, so if you are reflecting on a positive event, you can think about what you are still satisfied with or proud about.
- What were the effects of what I did or didn't do?
- What positives now emerge for me from the event?

- What have I noticed about my general behaviour in practice now I have had a chance to reflect on it?
- What are the key themes from the experience to explore in the literature?
- If relevant, what does anyone helping me to reflect on my practice have to say about my behaviour at the time?

Now what? (the action part)

This is the part where you think about how you will change your future actions as a result of reflecting on this experience. Here you may want to consider actions you will take in your practice as well as identifying learning opportunities that you want to take up as a result of the reflection.

Ask yourself:

- What are the implications for me (if relevant, and others) in practice based on what I have described and reflected on?
- What difference would it make to my future practice if I chose to do nothing?
- Where can I get more information to prepare me for a similar situation?
- How could I modify practice if a similar situation was to happen again?
- What help do I need to help me act on my learning from this reflection?
- Which aspect should be tackled first?
- How will I notice if I have improved my practice as a result of this reflection?
- What is the main learning that I take from reflecting on my practice?

Benefits and limitations of the What?, So what?, Now what? approaches

The three questions are straightforward and easy to remember when you are in practice. They are also general enough to suit most contexts. The additional questions in each provide clear cues for reflection.

However, because of the generalised nature of the questions you may need to adapt them to suit your purposes. It may seem that the questions are asking you to assume that the reflection is based on a negative experience, but you should remember that learning can take place from reflecting on positive experiences as well. Driscoll (2007) also notes that because of the emphasis on outcomes in this approach, you should ensure you do not neglect other elements of reflection such as description, emotion, or analysis.

Structuring an assignment based on a What? approach

Unless your lecturer has specified a particular structure, it's up to you whether you decide to focus on a topic in each section and include the answers to the three questions in each section, or whether you have three separate sections of the main body split into what/so what and now what? In any case you would need a separate introduction and conclusion to the assignment (see Chapters 9 through 11 for more information on assignment structure).

Read the following extracts from a social work student's assignment divided into What?, So what?, and Now what? sections using Driscoll's model for structured reflection. The reflection focuses on a role play interview situation where the student was tasked with ascertaining the views of a 9-year-old child, Jenny, as part of an assessment of Jenny's foster care placement. Jenny had experienced abuse from her mother and this was her second foster care placement in two years after the previous foster carer became chronically ill and was no longer able to look after her. This information was given in the introduction to the assignment. The following extracts are from the main body of the assignment. The prompt questions are included in call out boxes and you will notice that they are answered more than once throughout the extracts. Note that these are extracts only and this is not a full assignment.

What?

I chose to reflect on this mock interview with an actor playing a child, 'Jenny', in foster care, as while I am aware of the importance of gaining details about a child's feelings as part of an assessment (Buckley et al., 2006), this was the first time I had been given the opportunity to practice this scenario. Immediately after the event, I felt I had not succeeded in gaining the required information and wanted to understand why this might be and how I could improve my practice in this area.

> What is the purpose of returning to this event?

I entered the room with Arlene, who, for the purposes of the role-play, was acting as my supervisor. When I first saw the actor playing Jenny, I was shocked at how bad her skin was – the burn marks from the abuse she had suffered from her mother were clearly visible. After this, I avoided looking at Jenny and asked the list of questions I had prepared for a structured interview. When I asked Jenny to tell me what her life in the foster family had been like in the past two months, she replied 'alright'. I then asked what she wanted the future to look like and she mumbled something I couldn't hear.

> What happened?

> What did I see and do? What was my reaction?

At this point Arlene took over. She first introduced herself to Jenny and explained that Jenny shouldn't worry and that we wanted to make sure she has all the things she needs to be healthy and happy along with some of the subjects that we might discuss.

Arlene said we would write the information down in a report to tell us if she needed some more help. She then asked Jenny to tell her about a normal day in the family's life and what she enjoyed doing most. She gave Jenny a sheet with daily activity pictures on that she could circle and use as prompts. Then she asked if there was anything Jenny didn't like. Jenny replied that she didn't like sprouts. While Arlene was asking Jenny the questions, she looked in her eyes in a friendly way and Jenny seemed happy with this. Arlene gave Jenny a sheet that said 'if I had three wishes, I would wish for...' and underneath a space for some pictures. Jenny drew a picture of the foster family and a house. She said that she wished she could stay forever. She drew a picture of a big dog lying on the floor, and said 'I wish Sam's dog would die because it is scary.' When we checked afterwards with the notes, it transpired that Sam was the foster father's brother who sometimes visited the house.

Who else was involved and what did these people do?

So what?

A key to effective service user-social worker relationships is effective communication. The complexity of communication with looked-after children became clear to me as I reflected on this situation and in particular the importance of child-centred communication (as noted by Bannister and Huntington, 2002). The three aspects of child-centred communication I focus on here are the importance of developing trust with children though transparency; the importance of body language; and different activities for communicating with children at different developmental stages.

What are the key themes from the literature to draw out from the experience?

What worked or didn't work about the experience?

It is imperative for social workers to be able to develop a relationship of trust with the looked-after children they are working with and one way of doing this is to be transparent in communicating the aims of a meeting. Jenny's reply to me 'alright', contrasted with her communication with Arlene, showed that I had not developed a satisfactory rapport with her that I needed to in order for her to trust me enough to tell me about the problems with the relative's dog. Jenny was worried about talking to us – indeed it was the first time she had spoken to us, so there was no reason for her to trust us. As noted by Morrison (2016), children may have a number of different professionals involved in their lives and there is no reason for the social worker to be viewed by the child as a trusted adult. Jenny did not initially mention the dog, perhaps because she thought it was something that might mean she would be taken away from the foster family as she had been moved from her previous foster family. Arlene was able to develop a rapport with Jenny and gain her trust. The preamble that Arlene gave at the start was key in helping Jenny to relax and feel comfortable in talking to us, whereas I had started asking my questions without any introduction or explanation, as I usually tend to do. As noted by Cossar, Brandon and Jordan (2011), it is essential for children not to be 'kept in the dark' and to have access to an appropriately worded copy of the child protection plan. Jenny needed to understand why we were there, whereas I had just assumed that she would already know what our role was.

What positive events now emerge for me from the event?

What were the effects of what I did or didn't do?

What have I noticed about my behaviour in general in practice now I have had a chance to reflect on it?

Another important aspect of communication in social worker's communication with children is body language (Ruch, 2014; Winter et al., 2016). While I had taken Jenny's nervousness to be embarrassment over the appearance of her skin, it was in fact more likely that she was feeling uncomfortable because I had avoided looking at her and that I was embarrassed. My feeling about this was confirmed in the debrief session I had with Arlene after the assessment. Arlene said that I had appeared embarrassed and Jenny had seemed to reflect this emotion. Arlene, appearing undisturbed and calmly looking into Jenny's eyes was important for Jenny, as was the fact that she looked away again while Jenny was drawing, taking the cues from Jenny as to what was a suitable level of eye contact. I now feel ashamed that I had prioritised my own discomfort over Jenny's feelings and not been able to use more responsive, respectful communication as advocated by Winter et al. (2016).

How did I feel at the time?

Was this different from how other people involved felt at the time?

If relevant, what does anyone helping me to reflect on my practice have to say about my behaviour at the time?

It is essential that a social worker is aware of and prepared to use a number of different methods for communicating with children and a social worker also needs to consider the different developmental ages of children (Winter et al., 2016). When I failed to elicit any detailed information from Jenny through my list of questions, Arlene was able to turn to the additional and age-appropriate resources she had prepared for assistance and in this way was successful in gaining more information from Jenny. O'Reilly and Dolan (2015) write about the importance of play in communicating with children. I was reminded of this when Jenny started to become animated as she talked about her three wishes. While I had read about the importance of play, how this might be put into practice became clear to me after reflecting on this situation.

Do I still feel 'troubled' if so, in what way?

What is the main learning that I take from reflection on my practice?

Now what?

The main implication resulting from this reflection is that I will pay more attention to how I can develop my communication skills for working with vulnerable children. This will help me to develop a relationship of trust with these service users and enable me to conduct more successful assessments in order to support those who depend on me. While I have a good working knowledge of theoretical issues around social worker/child communication, if I do not develop my own practical skills in this area, I will be unable to fully realise my role as a competent social worker. Specifically, in a similar situation in the future, I would first introduce myself to the child and clearly explain what we hoped to gain from exploring the service user's feelings and that we would write a report to help us plan what we were going to do. I would remember that however nervous or uncomfortable I am feeling, the child is feeling much more apprehensive, and I must do everything I can to make that child feel safe in disclosing information to us. I would pay more attention to my own body language and the body language of the child and make my communication (both verbal and nonverbal) more responsive and respectful. This will help to put the service user at ease and build a more trusting relationship. In the meantime, I will also research the subject of building positive relationships with children in child protection circumstances. In particular, I will explore the uses of play in communicating with vulnerable children

What are the implications for me (if relevant, and others) in practice based on what I have described and reflected on?

What difference does it make for my future practice if I chose to do nothing?

Which aspect should be tackled first?

Where can I get more information to face a similar situation again?

(for example, O'Reilly and Dolan, 2016) and add more play activities to my own repertoire of communication skills. For example, I feel that the use of puppets for exploring emotions may have added even more to this scenario and it is something I will try in future. In order to understand whether I am successful in developing my communication skills with vulnerable children, I will work with my mentor in observations as well as continuing to reflect on my own practice.

What help do I need to help me 'action' the results of my reflections?

How will I notice if I am any different in practice?

In this example, the student is able to pick up and explain the information she provided in the *What?* section. She does this through linking the event and her feelings to themes from the literature. She closes the circle by stating how she would act in such a situation in the future, thus emphasising the development of her practice.

2 Gibbs' Reflective Cycle (1988)

This next approach includes many of the same elements as Driscoll's model, but the cycle is divided into six distinct steps. These steps are: Description, Evaluation, Thoughts and Feelings, Analysis, Conclusion and Action Plan. Gibbs' Reflective Cycle is one of the most commonly cited and used frameworks for reflection in healthcare, though it was originally developed in an educational context rather than for reflecting on healthcare practice.

The steps in the cycle are shown in Figure 6.1.

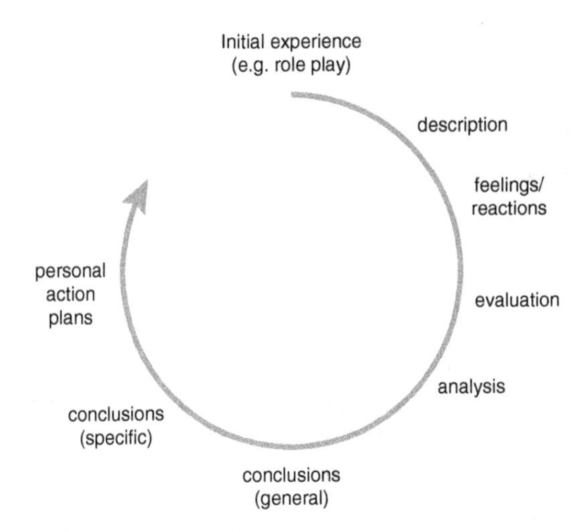

Figure 6.1 Gibbs' Reflective Cycle
(Gibbs, 1988:50)

Your lecturers will have expectations of exactly what they expect you to include at each of the stages, but answering the following questions can help you to find the information you will need.

Description

This is your description of the events. Here, don't include any description of how you felt about the events – thoughts and feelings come later. This really is description at the most basic level.

Ask:

- What happened?
- Who was there?
- What was my role in the events?
- What happened next?

See this as the story of what happened. Describe each separate action in chronological order or according to theme. This will provide a useful guide for you to return to throughout the rest of the assignment.

Thoughts and feelings

This is where you discuss how you felt at various times during the event.

Ask:

- How did I feel before the event?
- How did I feel during the event?
- How did I feel after the event?

Evaluation

This is where you write about the positive and negative elements of the event.

Ask:

- What worked?
- What aspects were positive?
- What didn't work?
- What aspects weren't positive?

Analysis

This is where you introduce the theory/literature and think about what each of the previous sections mean. (This section will likely make up the largest part of your assignment.)

Ask:

- Why did this happen?
- Why did I behave in this way?

- What have I learned?
- How does theory, policy or legislation relate to the events that I have already written about (use specific examples from the events)?

Conclusion

What you include here will depend on the guidelines you are given by your lecturer. There may be a conclusion to the reflection and then another conclusion to the assignment as a whole. In this case, some questions that can help you with your reflection conclusion are:

- What have I learned?
- What else could I have done?
- What might I do differently next time?
- What did I learn about myself?
- What did I learn about my own knowledge and practice?

Action plan

This is where you discuss how what you have learned during the reflection process will influence your practice in the future and what action you intend to take in the meantime.

Ask:

- If the same situation arose again, what could I do?
- What action can I take in the meantime to prepare for similar future situations?
- Even if the experience was positive and I did well, in which areas can I improve?
- What specific action can you take to improve in these areas?

Benefits and limitations of Gibbs' Reflective Cycle

This approach allows you to clearly structure your reflection. The separation into different aspects of the reflective process means that it is easy to ensure you cover all the relevant information.

However, some argue that it can be repetitive, and splitting the process into so many steps can oversimplify it, thus leading to a loss of depth in reflection (Jasper, 2013). Jasper notes too that using this cycle can mean that you stop at the action stage, as no exact same situation is likely to occur again, so the approach does not allow for the cycle to be closed. If you do choose to use this model, you need to ensure you achieve the right levels of critical analysis for the level of your course (see Chapters 12–14 for more information on critical analysis).

Structuring an assignment based on Gibbs' Reflective Cycle

Because there are six steps to this cycle, you might want to split your assignment into sections according to these steps. Note, you will need a separate introduction and conclusion to the assignment as a whole, so the conclusion to the assignment will be different from the conclusion within the reflective cycle. Another way to structure your assignment would be by dividing it by topic, with each of the steps addressed in every topic section.

EXERCISE 6.1

Try reorganising the elements from the social work student's assignment on pages 38–41 according to the six steps in Gibbs' Reflective Cycle. You may need to add some information. You don't need to write full sentences as in the previous examples – you can use bullet points. A few bullet points have been added already.

Description

Role-play – foster care child assessment

Entered the room

Appearance of child – burn marks

Thoughts and feelings

Evaluation

Analysis

Conclusion

Action plan

3 Kolb's Experiential Learning Cycle (1984)

By now, you'll have started to recognise that despite their different appearances, the approaches to reflection share a number of features. That's because they're all asking you to do basically the same thing: use reflection on your experiences as a learning tool for similar experiences in the future. The next approach we focus on, Kolb's Experiential Learning Cycle (1984), was also developed in an educational context as with Gibbs', and is widely used in healthcare settings. Kolb's Cycle (which is part of his Experiential Learning Theory) has four cyclical stages – you can begin at any point in the cycle, but you should follow the sequence of the stages. These stages are: Concrete Experience, Observation and Reflection, Forming Abstract Concepts, and Testing in New Situations. According to Kolb, the stage in your cycle from which you prefer to start will depend on what he calls your preferred learning style (for more information on learning styles, see, for example, Kolb, 1984; 2014). Despite the different labels to approaches we have looked at so far, the elements of the Experiential Learning Cycle should now seem somewhat familiar to you and you can probably guess what needs to be included in each stage.

Here is an overview of what to include in each stage, along with some questions that will help you ensure you include all the information you need at each stage.

Concrete experience (the description part)

This is where you describe the situation. In a similar way to '*What?*' in Driscoll's model and the description step in Gibbs' cycle, thoughts and feelings or reflections do not come into this part of your writing.

Ask:

- What happened?
- Who was there?
- What was my role in what happened?

Observation and reflection (the reviewing part)

This is the part where your reactions to the situation come in and where you start to think about what did or didn't go well, as well as the reasons for this.

Ask:

- What was positive/negative about the situation?
- Why did the events happen?
- Why did I behave as I did?
- Why did others behave in the way that they did?

Abstract conceptualisation (the theory part)

This is where you can incorporate theory from the literature and start to generalise from your situation.

Ask:

- What does the literature have to say about why the events happened?
- What can I learn from why I behaved as I did/why others behaved in the way that they did?

Active experimentation (the planning/trying out part)

Here you think about how what you have learned from the situation can be used to influence your practice and how you will change what you do in the future as a result of your reflections.

Ask:

- How can I change my practice based on my reflections on this experience?
- How have I changed my practice already based on my learning from these reflections?

Kolb's theory is visualised in Figure 6.2:

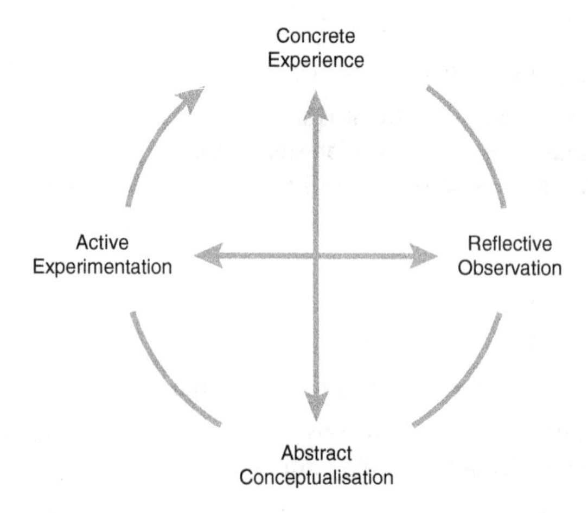

Figure 6.2 Kolb's Experiential Learning Cycle
(Kolb, 2014: 51)

Benefits and limitations of Kolb's Experiential Learning Cycle

One benefit of Kolb's cycle is its flexibility – it doesn't presume that things always happen in a certain order, so you can start at different stages. Because of the active experimentation stage, this cycle is highly suited to a 'learning by doing' approach. However, because of the flexibility of the approach, the approach can be confusing if you are new to reflection and would prefer something more structured.

Structuring an assignment based on Kolb's Experiential Learning Cycle

While the most obvious way to structure this piece of work will be to start with an introduction, followed by the concrete experience, and to continue through the stages, there may be a good reason to start at another of the stages. If you do this, ensure you explain why you are doing so in your introduction. You should also check the assignment guidelines from your lecturer carefully in case they have specified a particular order. As always, don't forget to include an introduction and conclusion for the assignment as well.

Comparing approaches to reflection

Table 6.1 gives an overview of the approaches to reflection we have outlined in this chapter.

EXERCISE 6.2

Try reorganising the elements from the student's assignment on pages 38–41 according to the four stages in Kolb's Experiential Learning Cycle. You may need to add some information. You don't need to write full sentences as in the examples – you can use bullet points as in the example already added.

Concrete experience

Entered the room

...

...

Observation and reflection

Abstract conceptualisation

Active experimentation

Table 6.1 Comparing approaches to reflection

Reflection approach and reference	Key components of reflection approach	Key prompts	Benefits/limitations of reflection approach
Borton (1970) Driscoll (2007) Rolfe et al. (2001)	**Description** **Analysis** **Action**	**What?** **So what?** **Now what?**	+ Easy to remember prompts. Flexible – will suit many contexts. – General questions means they may need adapting.
Gibbs (1998)	**Description** **Evaluation** **Thoughts and feelings** **Analysis** **Conclusion** **Action plan**	**What happened?** **What was good/bad?** **How did I feel?** **What does it mean?** **What is my main learning from this?** **What will I do now?**	+ Splits reflection into 6 clear steps, so it's easy to ensure you have included everything you need to. – Only asks you to reflect on the same situation occurring again, so you will need to bring in elements of another approach if you want to fully close the cycle. Can be repetitive. Lack of depth of reflection possible with some other approaches.
Kolb (1984)	**Concrete experience** **Reflective observation** **Abstract conceptualisation** **Active experimentation**	**What happened?** **Why did it happen?** **What does it mean?** **What will I do now/what have I done?**	+ Highly suited to practice and encourages you to try out learning. – Flexibility of approach may make it difficult for those new to reflection.

EXERCISE 6.3

While we have outlined some approaches to reflection, in order to gain a thorough understanding of how they work in practice you will need to try using them. Choose a recent memorable event that has happened to you and work your way through the questions at each stage by noting bullet points and moving them around/adding to them where necessary for each of the three approaches (for Driscoll, for Gibbs and for Kolb). You can choose an event that happened on placement, something that has happened in your studies or something else entirely, such as a car breakdown or a family party that didn't go as expected. The key here is to practice using the approaches. Try using all three of the approaches and note which one gives you a deeper understanding of the event.

TIP

Choose a different approach to work with each week while on placement.

Noting down your experiences from placement every day will give you a wealth of material to work with once you come to writing your assignments. You will thank your earlier self if you start making this your routine now!

Summary

- Use a recognised model, cycle or framework to structure your reflection
- Practice using the different approaches to capture your reflections
- Signal in your writing which approach you are using and why
- Incorporate all the elements of the approach in your assignment

CHAPTER

7

Planning

By the end of this chapter, you should be able to:

- Understand how to effectively manage your time in order to complete reflective assignments by the deadline
- Use techniques to help you plan the structure of your reflective assignment

Managing your time

As a nursing, health or social work student, you will soon find that your schedule becomes very busy. Not only will you be out on placement, but in no time you will have assignment deadlines looming as well. Learning how to manage your time effectively to get these assignments done will have huge benefits. Not only will you feel less stressed, but you will very likely achieve higher marks.

In this chapter, we have outlined some of the most important and relevant points that will help you complete your reflective assignments.

Start early

With any assignment, you will maximise your chances of success by starting work as soon as you can. It's all too easy to procrastinate and leave it to the last minute (and most students will do this at least once), but getting into the habit of beginning your first draft when you get your assignment title will serve you well throughout your course. (This is why keeping a reflective journal is such a good idea, as the incident you decide to focus on might already be recorded.)

You may have heard the idea that a good essay isn't written, it's rewritten. Reflective assignments are a process of organising your thoughts, tying up themes, and seeing how your experiences link to the literature. This is a complex task, and therefore your writing will almost certainly benefit from a number of drafts.

Successful students often adopt a process of finishing a draft, then leaving it for a number of days before returning to it with fresh eyes. The time away from writing will allow you to see errors you hadn't noticed, or to see new connections between ideas. Of course, to implement this effective strategy, you'll need the *time* to do it.

Set micro goals

Many students find the process of sitting down to write an assignment extremely daunting. It can be quite demoralising, struggling with an assignment for days and realising you are only halfway through. Learning to break the big task – for example, a 4,000-word assignment – down into a series of much smaller tasks is one way to help solve both problems.

Think about each of the different 'micro tasks' you need to do in order to complete the assignment. Instead of seeing 'research' as just one job, think of every paper you have to read as an individual step. Likewise, don't think about the overall task of writing 4,000 words, but focus on just one section – or even just one paragraph – at a time. Again, the more 'little wins' you can make happen along the way, the more motivated you'll feel to keep going.

Make each task a separate goal. The more specific about these goals you can be the better. Setting yourself a target of, for example, completing your introduction or writing 250 words in a day gives you a very definite goal to aim for. Not only does this feel achievable and less daunting than sitting down to write a whole assignment, but completing your goal for the day feels good, and will keep you motivated. It's important that you make sure the goals you set for yourself are realistic – trying to do too much and not achieving it means you may become demotivated again.

Use stress to your advantage

There is a well-known principle in time management that 'work expands to fill the time allotted to it'. You may recognise this as true – when we have three weeks to write an assignment it will take three weeks. If we have just a weekend, we can do it in 48 hours! The reason? Our old friend stress kicks in and helps us get it done. Of course, you don't want to make yourself too stressed, and we are not suggesting that you try and do your assignment in a single weekend. But stress in small doses is actually quite a useful tool to help get things done. There is even a word for it: eustress.

To harness your eustress, try giving yourself 'mini' deadlines. For example, if you are working on a patchwork assignment, give each patch a due date. Again, be realistic when you do this about how long it will take.

Use the magic tomato

One well-known tool that makes use of many of the principles we've mentioned is known as the Pomodoro Technique. Pomodoro means 'tomato' in Italian, and the tomato is not a real one, but refers to a cooking timer that you might buy from a kitchenware shop.

The basic principle is this: set a timer to go off after a certain number of minutes (25 is recommended). Put it on your desk and start the timer. From that moment until the alarm rings, focus only on the task you have set yourself (200 words, for example).

When the timer goes off, stop. Stand up and take a 5- or 10-minute break. (Enough time to make a cuppa!) Then return and repeat.

For most people, three or four pomodoro sessions is enough before taking a longer break.

A quick internet search will help you find a lot more resources on this handy little tool, but it's an extremely useful one for nursing, health or social work students, who may have to fit writing around placements and family life.

Eliminate distractions

Distractions are a part of life, and there seem to be more than ever these days. Why would you sit down and write an assignment when you could be scrolling social media or watching funny videos on YouTube?

The problem is that all these distractions make it hard to focus on the work we have in front of us. They break our concentration, meaning the work takes longer and feels more difficult.

Removing these distractions may well be the single most effective step you take to help manage your time. Try turning your phone off when you sit down to study (turning it on again can be the 'reward' at the end of a pomodoro session!). If you can't turn it off, at least go into your settings and disable all notifications. That will stop your phone endlessly pinging at you as you try to work.

Know your body clock

Why is it that sometimes we can sit down and write 500 words in a morning, and other times we find ourselves staring at a page for hours, with nothing getting done? The answer may well lie in your body's circadian rhythm, or your 'body clock'. We all work better at different times; some people are sharper and more creative in the mornings, others take time to get going but often do their best work in the afternoon or even late at night.

You probably already know instinctively when you do your best work. Try and schedule your research and writing time around these hours where possible.

EXERCISE 7.1

A plan for tomorrow

Take a blank sheet of paper. Write the hours of the day, divided into 30-minute slots, down the left-hand side of the page.

Now think of your day tomorrow. Write in all the commitments you know you have already such as work, and/or picking up the children. In the spare time, plan four pomodoro sessions dedicated to study time.

Set very specific goals such as word counts for each slot. (Don't forget to make these achievable.)

Schedule the times for when you know you have the most energy, and will be least distracted.

Try the plan tomorrow and monitor how it works for you.

Planning your reflective assignment

The first step of planning your writing is to read your question carefully and consider **what** it is asking and **how** you will answer it – doing this will help you to understand your assignment's structure. Becoming aware of your assignment's overall structure will enable you to keep your answer 'on track' and help manage your time, reading, and your stress levels – as well as helping you to achieve higher marks!

For the purposes of illustration, consider the following question:

Critically discuss one key aspect of the NMC Code of Practice and relate this to your professional development through reflecting on your experiences on the ward.

To identify what the question is asking and how you will answer it, you must first find the **topic(s)** and **instruction word(s)** present in the question. This can be done be underlining and highlighting only the words which answer the questions:

- *What* should I write about? (Topic) underline your answers
- *How* should I write about it? (Instruction) *highlight your answers*

In the example question, you may identify the answer to these questions and underline them as such:

Critically discuss **one key aspect of the NMC Code of Practice and relate this to your professional development through reflecting on your experiences on the ward.**

In this example, the question instructs you to critically discuss: this is *how* you are expected to answer. It also guides you to write about one aspect (not two, or three!) of the NMC Code of Practice in terms of your professional development. As with all reflective assignments, you should use your experiences to inform your answer.

TIP

Note: not all assignments will include an explicit instruction word

Sometimes, they may simply ask you to reflect; however, in any assignment you should still be able to answer the two first questions of planning. Most assignments will require critical analysis, so consider the word 'reflect' as including this skill.

The next step to overall planning is to brainstorm. Get a piece of paper (or a blank word-processing document if you prefer) and try to empty your mind of your ideas prompted by the question. At the brainstorming stage, there are no wrong answers – this a useful step that is just for you. You can decide what is relevant later. Once you have brainstormed, the next thing you should do is to create your living plan as in Figure 7.1. Remember that this is called a living plan because it will change as you do more reading and research – you might add more sections or decide that some are not required as you study.

Figure 7.1 shows a living plan in its first draft. The percentages next to each section relate to the rough proportion of your assignment's word count which you should dedicate to each part. More detail on what to include in the introduction is in Chapter 9; the body paragraphs should follow a structure as outlined in Chapters 10, 12 and 13; and information on writing conclusions is included in Chapter 11. Just getting an idea of how many words to use on each part of your assignment will mean that you can break down the task of writing into smaller tasks. Remember that the structure of your assignment may depend on the approach you choose for reflection – for example, if after reading Chapter 6, you decide to use Gibbs' reflective model, then the different stages of reflection would make up the different sections of the main body of your assignment.

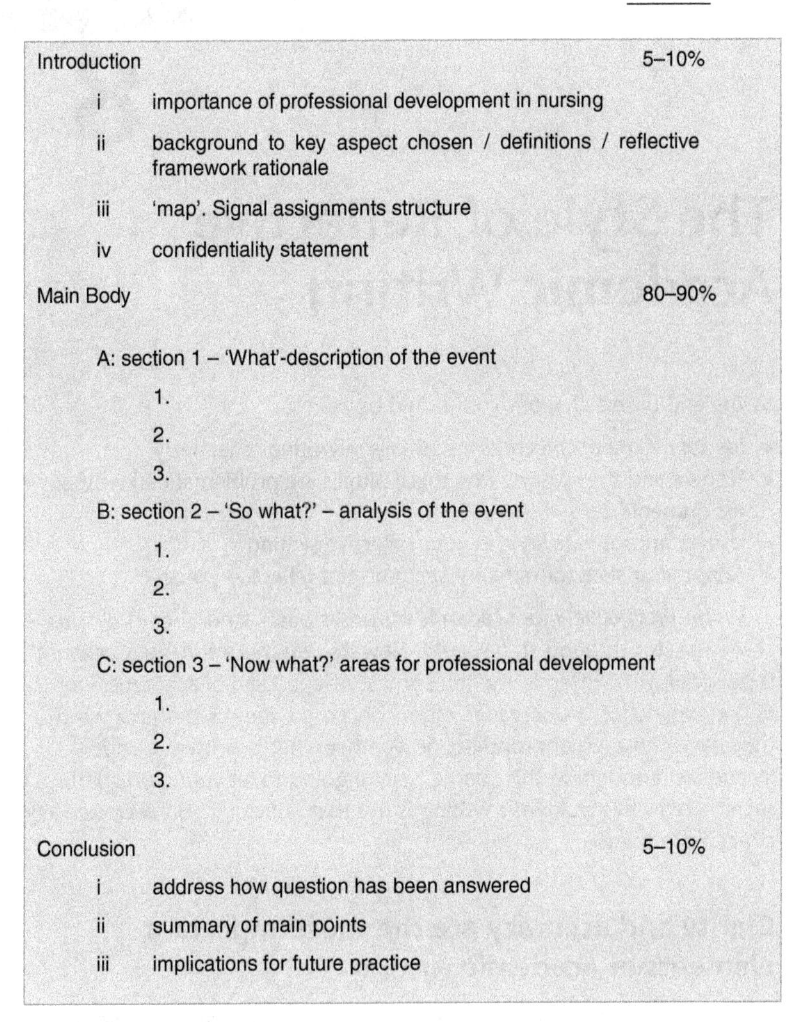
Introduction 5–10%

i importance of professional development in nursing

ii background to key aspect chosen / definitions / reflective framework rationale

iii 'map'. Signal assignments structure

iv confidentiality statement

Main Body 80–90%

A: section 1 – 'What'-description of the event

1.
2.
3.

B: section 2 – 'So what?' – analysis of the event

1.
2.
3.

C: section 3 – 'Now what?' areas for professional development

1.
2.
3.

Conclusion 5–10%

i address how question has been answered

ii summary of main points

iii implications for future practice

Figure 7.1 Making an overall 'living' plan

Summary

- Managing your time effectively is important
- Removing distractions and understanding when and how you work best will help you
- Creating and using a living plan will help you to set realistic goals when writing

CHAPTER

8

The Style of Reflective Academic Writing

By the end of this chapter, you should be able to:

- Identify some of the common pitfalls in writing reflectively
- Understand the reasons why these pitfalls are problematic in written assignments
- Use an appropriate style in your reflective writing
- Adapt your style for different sections of a reflective piece

Writing reflectively for academic purposes poses a number of difficult challenges for students to navigate. How do you make sure your account is personal, yet written in the tone and style expected of academic work? In our experience, students are often concerned about whether a word they have chosen is appropriate, or whether what is written sounds 'academic' enough. In this chapter, we're going to let you in on a little secret – reflective academic writing is not that difficult if you keep two key concepts in mind:

Clarity and accuracy are the most important elements of academic writing

- using big words that 'sound academic' is not necessarily good practice
- longer sentences don't always mean better developed ideas

If you make your writing clear, the ideas you are trying to communicate to your reader will be understood as you intend. A skilful writer will consider their use of words and 'fine tune' their work so that it narrows (or eliminates) the possibility for misunderstanding.

The four principles of reflective academic writing

When you are asked to write reflectively, it is common to ask yourself questions such as 'Should I use "I" in my writing?' and 'How can I write academically *and* reflectively?' These and other frequently asked questions are answered in this chapter, but a key point to remember here is that reflective writing **is** academic writing – it still needs to be clear.

To help you achieve this clarity, there are four key principles which you can remember. These are: use formal language, make every sentence count, be concise, and present your ideas logically. Each of these will now be considered in more detail.

Use formal language

When writing in a reflective way, it can be easy to slip into what we might call a 'stream of consciousness' style of writing. A student may use reflection as a form of diary entry and because of this, their word choice may be more informal than they may otherwise use in a 'normal' (non-reflective) assignment. The resulting writing can be disorganised, closer to everyday speech than to academic writing, and often lacking the clarity necessary to score highly. It is important to distinguish between the style of writing you might use in your diary entries while in practice (see Chapter 4), and reflective writing that you will use in written assignments.

Keep in mind that all rules of formality originate from the key point: *are ideas clearly expressed?*

Table 8.1 shows some of the key differences between everyday speech and academic writing and gives you some questions to ask yourself so you can avoid your reflective writing becoming too diary-like.

Table 8.1 Everyday speech vs academic writing

Everyday speech	Academic writing	Ask	Avoid
Conversational language	Uses formal vocabulary and correct terminology	Is there a more formal way of saying this?	Slang (*kids*) Phrasal or two-part verbs (get up/get bigger).
The kids came along too.	*The children accompanied the patient.*		Idioms *(under the weather, slept like a baby).*
She was clearly feeling under the weather.	*It was evident she was feeling unwell.*		

(continued)

Table 8.1 (continued)

Everyday speech	Academic writing	Ask	Avoid
Is more wordy and repetitive *During my preparation for ward rounds that day, I had prepared ward round reports and in doing so, had sat with all patients to ascertain their views and wishes in addition to any requests they wanted to ask as they did not want to represent themselves in the meeting.*	Is clear and concise *I prepared ward round reports by sitting with all patients to ascertain their views and wishes. I noted any requests from patients who did not want to represent themselves in the meeting.*	Have I said the same thing more than once? Are there any words that don't need to be there because the meaning is clear from the context? Could I use shorter sentences?	Using two words where you could use one.
Is often vague *It was really good.*	Is precise *There were several positive aspects to the care.*	Is this precise? Does it state exactly what I want to say?	Things/stuff/ good/bad.

Example of informal writing

In the following example, a nursing student describes his feelings during his chosen reflection event. Highlighted in bold are examples where the language is too informal. Explanations and suggested alternatives are given in the box on the right.

Informal version

I have to admit I wasn't really looking forward *to* ***carrying out*** *the assessment on* **Mr Harvey – the** *handover nurse had mentioned his pressure ulcers and* ***if I'm honest*** *these are the one thing I still* ***find hard to handle. My heart was in my mouth*** *as I entered the room and introduced myself.*

Explanations

I have to admit – Colloquial phrases we might use when speaking aren't necessary in academic writing, even when we are writing about our own experiences.

I wasn't really looking forward.
Avoid contractions;
the adverb 'really' – it doesn't (really) add anything to the meaning of the sentence;
'looking forward' and carrying out' are both two-part verbs; that is, verbs made of a verb and a preposition. There are hundreds of these in English, but there is almost always a one-word alternative. In most cases this one-word alternative will more accurately describe the action.

Hard to handle This is an example of metaphorical language, which is generally not appropriate in academic writing. Why not? Because the literal meaning is different from the intended one.

if I'm honest This is another example where the language used is more appropriate for spoken than written English.

Mr Harvey – The dash is used extensively these days in email and text language, often to connect two ideas or signify a change of direction in a sentence. It is not always considered academic and should be avoided in your writing.

My heart was in my mouth – This is an example of a cliché – a common phrase with a meaning that most people will understand, though if we consider the literal meaning it does not accurately describe the situation (thankfully so, in this example!)

Remember, effective writing eliminates the possibility of misunderstanding by being as precise and concise as possible.

Revised version	Changes made
I was feeling apprehensive *about* ***conducting*** *the assessment on Mr Harvey. The handover nurse had mentioned his pressure ulcers and this is one condition thing I still* ***find difficult. I felt nervous*** *as I entered the room and introduced myself.*	***I have to admit*** has been deleted.
	Wasn't could be changed to was not, but instead a positive statement is used. ***Really*** has been deleted, The two-part or phrasal verb ***carry out*** has been changed to the single verb ***conducting***.
	The phrase **if I'm honest** has been deleted.
	The dash has been changed to a full stop. Other alternatives would be a comma or a semicolon. NB: There is one more punctuation mark which is not usually acceptable in academic writing. Can you guess what it is...?
	The cliché ***my heart was in my mouth*** has been replaced with ***I felt nervous***.

EXERCISE 8.1

The following paragraph from the Description section of a reflective essay has several examples of informal language. Find the examples and choose the best correction from the box.

If you feel an entire sentence or clause is too informal and no alternative exists you may choose to delete it entirely.

The head nurse was running a bit late for Mr. Barnard's morning injection. I was at a loose end so I went in to his cubicle and had a chat with him for 5 or 6 minutes until the nurse arrived. I made small talk, asking things like how his day had been and which TV programmes he liked to watch. Then I noticed he came over a bit funny. His speech got slower then he just started to stutter, just going over the same sounds over and over again, then finally his head dropped to his chest and he stopped talking altogether. I stuck my head out of the cubicle but the head nurse was nowhere to be seen so I called out for help. Then it struck me that there was a panic button right next to Mr. Barnard's bed. That was really stupid of me to forget that. I ran up to the button and pressed it. It was all a bit of a blur, but I picked up Mr. Barnard's head from his chest and checked his ABC. He was still breathing and there was no blockage. Two senior nurses came into the room and I told them everything what I knew and they took over. I stepped back and watched and as I did Mr. Barnard came round. The nurses asked him questions like could he remember the day and things like that, which he answered correctly.

Talked	Stepped out of the cubicle	That
Such as	I asked	Regained consciousness
He began to stutter	I remembered	Behind schedule
A short time	Airway, Breathing and Circulation	
I had arrived before her		A change in his demeanour

Make every sentence count

You need to make sure every sentence 'does a job' and you are not repeating yourself. Watch out for repetition in your writing in a couple of different ways. Firstly, make sure that you're not repeating language too often – effective writing varies everything from vocabulary to sentence length to the grammatical structures used.

Consider this example from an Introduction to a nursing assignment:

This essay will focus on the subject of dignity and how dignity can be maintained within a healthcare setting. Dignity is defined by the RCN (2008) as 'how people think, feel and behave in relation to the worth or value of themselves and others.' When considering dignity within a healthcare setting it is useful to note that there are many different ways in which a patient's dignity can be upheld (Warner, 2005). These include ensuring good communication, maintaining privacy and encouraging autonomy.

It won't take long reading this to realise that the student is repeating the keyword 'dignity' a little too often. When we read this it jars somehow – disrupting the flow of the text.

So how can we avoid this mistake – especially when the word we are repeating is the subject of our assignment?

A few solutions might be:

1 Use pronouns

Those little words such as 'it', 'they' and 'these' can be used when it is clear (usually thanks to a previous sentence) exactly what we are writing about.

For example:

This essay will focus on the subject of **dignity** and how <u>**it**</u> can be maintained within a healthcare setting.

2 Use synonyms

Words that share a similar meaning to the key term can be used to make your writing more varied.

For example:

One **issue** faced by healthcare professionals is maintaining privacy when in a busy ward. The **problem** can be resolved to some extent by...

3 Use 'umbrella terms'

These are broad terms that state what the subject you are writing about is. Idea, theory, practice, regulation etc.

For example:

Dignity is important for everyone. When considering **the idea** within a healthcare setting...

Watch out for:

It's not just the words you use that should avoid repeating. Writing can also become jarring to read if:

- **Too many sentences are of similar length**. Aim to mix up your sentence lengths within a paragraph to keep an interesting rhythm. Try using this pattern: short sentence, long sentence, short sentence, long sentence.
- **Too many sentences have a similar grammatical structure.** Just like words being repeated, it can soon become irritating if every sentence follows the same pattern.
- **Paragraphs start with the same word or grammatical structure.** Yes, our ear will even pick up when repetition occurs between paragraphs. Remember – variety is the spice of good writing!

The second kind of repetition concerns the same idea expressed in more than one way. This highlights a key difference between spoken and written English; when we talk we use many different kinds of techniques to emphasise points and keep our listener's attention. We often express the same idea in many different ways. This is natural as we seem to understand instinctively that most people are fairly poor listeners and we repeat ourselves to make sure our point is understood. In writing, we have the opportunity to be more concise. While effective writing will emphasise and maintain attention also, the techniques used by a skilled writer are different from techniques for speaking.

Repetition can be an easy trap for a writer to fall into. Sometimes a lack of planning, or not editing work will result in a writer using the same words again and again. As well as repeated words, it is important for the writer to engage with the meaning of what they are writing. If ideas are repeated, this will also pose issues unless the writer acknowledges the repetition.

This kind of repetition is particularly common when bringing in literature around your subject. Consider the following extract from an essay reflecting on a critical incident:

> *The decision to bring the patient into immediate care was made due to the extreme distress they were exhibiting. Parlor and Thyer (2003) state that when a patient is deemed to be a risk to themselves or others, the appropriate action for a social worker to take is to bring them into care immediately. Jameson (2007) notes that a patient must be admitted into care at the first sign that they may harm themselves or their family. The RCN (2008) policy decrees 'when a person is deemed to be dangerous, either to themselves or others, appropriate action is to undergo appropriate procedures for their admission to hospital as soon as possible'.*

In this example, the student has repeated the same idea several times, without building on the idea or showing how they link. While it is important to bring in a range of sources, you should aim to avoid repeating the same ideas.

An improved version of this might read:

> *The decision to bring the patient into immediate care was made due to the extreme distress they were exhibiting. This decision is commensurate with the literature on extreme distress in patients from within different healthcare professions. For example, Parlor and Thyer (2003) and Jameson (2007) both highlight that when a patient is deemed to be a risk to themselves or others, the appropriate action for a social worker to take is to bring them into care immediately. Likewise, from a nursing perspective, the RCN (2008) policy decrees "when a person is deemed to be dangerous, either to themselves or others, appropriate action is to undergo appropriate procedures for their admission to hospital as soon as possible".*

Be concise

If you feel (or have been told) that your work is 'wordy', it is likely that some of what you are writing is redundant. Put simply, redundancy is the use of words which do not contribute to or add to the idea expressed in the sentence you are writing. It can be tricky to identify redundancy in your work so it, like other aspects of study, requires practice. One key question to ask yourself at all times is: 'If I took this away, would it affect the meaning?' If the answer is no, you can safely adjust your text.

Consider the following from the Analysis section of a reflective essay. Highlighted in bold are examples of redundancy. Explanations and suggested alternatives are given in the table on the right.

*During the labour stage Mrs Beynon was experiencing extremely painful contractions, **which were a source of much discomfort and stress.** However, the head nurse did not consider the pain to be **too extreme in severity,** so the nursing team were told to provide reassurance. Clifton (2007) states that one of the most important roles of the midwife is to help their patient feel comfortable. **Another point that Clinton also makes** is that a mother will find it easier to relax if the midwife is relaxed and calm in her demeanour.*	**which were a source of much discomfort and stress –** As the writer has already noted the contractions were 'extremely painful' it goes without saying that they also caused discomfort and stress. Remember the key question: If I took this away would the meaning be lost? In this case it wouldn't, so the entire clause can be deleted.
	too extreme in severity – This is a common error in academic writing; the student has given us unnecessary information. In this case it's unnecessary for the writer to tell us how they are measuring pain, and for pain to be extreme it will always be severe as well.
	another point that Clinton also makes – Another and also have the same meaning – the student need only use one of the two words.

Revised version	Changes made
*During the labour stage Mrs Beynon was experiencing extremely painful contractions, However, the head nurse did not consider the pain to be **too severe** so the nursing team were told to provide reassurance. Clifton (2007) states that one of the most important roles of the midwife is to help their patient feel comfortable. **Another point that Clinton makes** is that a mother will find it easier to relax if the midwife is relaxed and calm in her demeanor.*	***which were a source of much discomfort and stress –*** The clause has been deleted without a loss of meaning.
	too extreme in severity – This has been changed to **too severe** as this covers the meaning without any redundancy.
	also has been deleted.

Present your ideas logically

Academic writing is highly predictable. There are certain elements of effective academic writing structure that lecturers will expect to see in all assignments. These include introductions, conclusions and clear paragraphing. Reflective writing is often even more prescriptive in its structure than many other types of writing. This is good news, because it means it makes it easier for you to write your assignment. If you follow the advice on planning, structure, and approaches to reflective writing in Chapters 6 to 11 you should be on the right path.

Style in different sections of reflective assignments

As discussed already, even though this is a reflective assignment and you need to reflect on your own experiences, it still needs to be written in academic *style*. This means that your lecturers will expect to see writing that:

- Is more formal than everyday speech
- Is clear and easy to understand
- Uses correct terminology

Each section of your assignment explains a different aspect of your experience. Depending on which reflective approach you are using, these sections will be in a different order (see Chapter 6 for frameworks, models and cycles of reflective writing). Whichever approach you use, you need to think carefully about which style to use in each section (Table 8.2).

Should I use I?

Yes, this is a reflective piece of writing, and you are expected to write about your own experiences and what you have learned from them. However, some elements of the essay will require more of a focus on your own experiences (using I) and some more on the literature (avoiding personal pronouns like *I/we* by using third person and passive voice – see Chapter 13 for an explanation of the *passive voice*).

Table 8.2 Elements of a reflective assignment using Gibbs' and different language features

Elements of assignment	Content	Example sentence	Notes on style	Main tense(s)*
Introduction	Aim/structure of assignment Choice of framework Confidentiality statement.	*This essay shows how my understanding of the concept of dignity was deepened through reflecting on my experiences in a clinical placement.*	Some use of the first person ('I'), but not overly – you are not reflecting yet.	Present (*this essay discusses*) or future (will tense: *this essay will discuss*).
Description	What happened.	*The supervisor pulled the curtains around the patient's bed.*	Mainly in the first person. Avoid evaluation/analysis.	Past or 'narrative' tenses (*we entered the ward*).
Thoughts and feelings	How *you* felt.	*I felt apprehensive when we first entered the patient's bedroom.*	Write this in the first person and include adjectives to describe your emotions *(apprehensive/satisfied)*	Past or narrative tenses to talk about how you felt. (*I felt apprehensive*).
Evaluation	What went well. What could have gone better.	*One satisfactory element of care communication with the patient's family.*	Though this is an evaluation, it needs to be written objectively (or fairly) and precisely. How was it good/bad etc.? What was good or bad? You may use 'I' to write about what happened while you were there, but to *evaluate* these events, try to avoid the first person. This will make your evaluations more objective.	Past or narrative tenses to talk about how things were *(One satisfactory aspect of care was communication. The nurses explained to the family what was going to happen next).* 3rd conditionals to discuss what could have been better: (*one element of care that could have been improved was).*

Analysis	Relate your experiences to the themes from the literature,	*Another important aspect of dignity that nurses need to consider is that of a patient's autonomy (ref)*	You will need to refer to your own experiences in the first person. This will predominantly not be in the first person as the focus is on how these relate to the key themes in the literature.	Present tense to talk about what is true (privacy *is* an important aspect of). Passive Tenses to discuss concepts. *(Communication <u>is regarded</u> by many as the most important skill a nurse can learn)*
Conclusion	Highlight what you have learned through the refection process by briefly pulling out the key themes identified. Some assignments require an additional conclusion to the reflective process.	*In sum, through reflecting on an instance from my own practice on the ward, this essay has shown the importance of upholding both the physical and relational aspects of dignity and highlighted the fact that the two cannot be separated.*	A mix of first person and passives in your conclusion to switch between talking about your experiences and the process of reflection.	Present perfect have *tense (this essay has shown/I have gained a deeper understanding)* to talk about what you have learned.
Action plan	What you have learned from the reflective process and how this will affect your practice going forward.	*I will continue to reflect on my experiences in practice through engaging with relevant literature.*	Mainly in the first person.	Future tense *(will).*

*These are the main tenses that you might like to use in each section.

EXERCISE 8.2

The following paragraph from the analysis section of a reflective essay contains several areas that could be stylistically improved. Find examples of the following:

Informality	**Repetition of Words**
Repetition of Ideas	**Redundancy**

(NB: You may find more than one example for each)

The chaotic scene at the home when we arrived meant that all members of the paramedic team were required to be aware of their body language. Jason and Humphreys (2014) state that body language is a powerful form of communication and that we can detect what another person feels within a matter of seconds. Obviously, it is therefore important not to give off body language that suggests negative feelings towards a patient. Marsden (2006) states that this may cause them to put up an instant barrier. Jones (2004) suggests that negative body language can cause patients to feel reluctant to communicate with a paramedic. In order to avoid causing these negative feelings from the outset, Johnson (2009) states that a paramedic should adopt neutral body language, which does not convey negative feelings. He states that the spine should be straight, the shoulders relaxed and that eye contact should be maintained while talking (Johnson, 2009). This creates an environment in which the paramedic can then begin to break down some of the more challenging communication barriers.

Now turn to the back of the book to check your answers.

Informality

Repetition of Words

Repetition of Ideas

Redundancy

CHAPTER

9

Introductions for Reflective Assignments

By the end of this chapter, you should be able to:

- Understand the purpose of introductions
- Identify the main functional elements of introductions
- Write interesting and purposeful introductions

First impressions count

You may have heard that first impressions are important; well, the introduction is your chance to make a good first impression on your reader, and as such *it is* important. A well-written introduction will contextualise your reflective assignment, demonstrate its value, and eliminate surprises by guiding your reader through an overview of the assignment. In order to write purposeful introductions, you should consider the following:

How long should an introduction be?

While there is no definitive answer to this question, most introductions will typically comprise between 5% and 10% of your total word count (see the 5–10% note in Figure 9.1). This means that if you are required to write a 4,000-word reflective assignment, you could initially aim to use between 200 and 400 words on the introduction.

What should my introduction include?

There are four functions to consider when you are writing an introduction and you can include these in whichever order works best for you. For clarity, these four functions are explored (and link to points i, ii, iii and iv in Figure 9.1):

i. *Demonstrate the relevance of your topic for reflection.* Although it may sound cynical, first start with the question: 'what is the point?' Imagine that you are trying to convince a stubborn friend as to why

Figure 9.1 A plan of an introduction

they should bother reading this piece of work. Here, you may find it useful to consider what information could be included to help support you when convincing this friend. Now, when reading for your assignment you can label any information that could help support you in convincing this friend with **Int-i** (see function i in Figure 9.1). This will help you as you come to write, as the more logical you can be when reading, the more logical your writing will be.

ii. *Contextualise your assignment.* Provide a background to your topic and your reflection. You may want to include key definitions, a brief history of your area of study or an overview of the main arguments present in relevant literature. While reading, when you find information which is useful in providing this context, you can label it **Int-ii.**

iii. *Eliminate surprise by guiding your reader through the rest of your assignment.* This statement is very much like the announcement at the beginning of a train journey: state all the points that the assignment will address in their order of appearance. Pay particular attention to your question here: make sure that you are clearly showing your reader how the set question will be answered and the order in which the information appears. Which approach to reflection are you using? You may also want to provide a rationale for using the chosen framework, model or cycle. Due to the nature of this function, it is unlikely that you will need to use the label **Int-iii** on any literature you're reading.

iv. *Include any other statements which your assignment guidelines require.* For example, you may need to include a confidentiality statement. Like function iii, you may not be able to label any literature with **Int-iv,** but that doesn't make it any less important. Indeed, these kinds of statements can often be vital for inclusion in your assignment. Check your assignment guidelines for further instruction.

Although the plan labels these elements separately, you don't have to write them as separate paragraphs.

EXERCISE 9.1

Read the introduction and identify where the four functions of the introduction are.

Dignity is a key concept in nursing and integral to the Nursing and Midwifery Code of Practice. The NMC states that in prioritising people, its members should 'Treat people as individuals and uphold their dignity' (NMC, 2018).

Dignity is a complex concept which can be viewed from different perspectives. The Royal College of Nursing defines dignity as *'concerned with how people feel, think and behave in relation to the worth or value of themselves and others. To treat someone with dignity is to treat them as being of worth, in a way that is respectful of them as valued individuals'* (RCN, 2008), thus alluding to both the physical and relational aspects of dignity. Research has suggested that while elderly patients and their relatives place more importance on the physical aspects of care in upholding dignity, healthcare professionals often place more value on the relational aspects (Cairns et al., 2013). There are many competing demands on a nurse's time, and the nurse needs to ensure that both physical and relational dignity remain at the forefront of care, even when under time and other pressures.

This essay discusses the importance of holistic care in upholding dignity and recognises that the physical and the relational elements of dignity cannot be separated. It does this by means of reflecting on an event from my placement on a geriatric ward caring for a 92-year-old diabetic amputee. I consider how my understanding of the concept of dignity has been deepened through this reflection. Specifically, I consider dignity as under the NMC code of conduct. The following three elements of upholding dignity are explored: treating patients with compassion; recognising diversity and individual choice and delivering the fundamentals of care. Through this lens I pinpoint emotional intelligence, confidence and decision-making abilities as key areas for my own personal development in order to provide holistic care that upholds dignity.

I use the *What? So what? Now what?* reflection framework put forward by Driscoll (2007), as this allows a clear means of structuring my essay with a number of trigger questions to guide the reflection process.

In accordance with the NMC (2015), all names have been replaced with pseudonyms.

TIP – REVISIT

Your introduction after you have written your assignment to consider whether you have indicated the main points covered in the work. If you need to make things clearer for your reader, don't hesitate to rework your introduction

Summary

- There are four main functions which should be addressed in an introduction to a written piece of reflective work
- Make an approximate word allowance for an introduction (about 5–10% of the word count)
- Revisit your introduction to ensure that it accurately guides the reader through your assignment

CHAPTER

10

Paragraphs for Reflective Assignments

By the end of this chapter, you should be able to:

- Recognise the importance of paragraph structure
- Recognise elements of an effective paragraph
- Write clear paragraphs which develop logically

Applying logical structure to your writing

The body of your assignment is where you will provide your case study for reflection and analyse it. You may find that following one of the approaches to reflection in Chapter 6 can help you to structure the body of your assignment. Whatever framework, model or cycle you decide to follow, there is one thing all will have in common: the paragraphs you write within the assignment should be structured logically. To do this, remember that paragraphs exist to make your and your reader's lives easier. Each paragraph should address an idea and each sentence within a paragraph should logically follow the last. Although different paragraphs will be different lengths, if you have many paragraphs which are one or two sentences long, your work may (at least appear to) be underdeveloped. Conversely, if your assignment has only a few, very long paragraphs, you may need to think more carefully about how you separate your ideas.

Referring to Figure 10.1, the body paragraphs are indicated by the notes A1, A2, A3, etc.

If you are presenting a narrative at the start of your reflection, consider how you can make this as logical as possible. You may find it easier to write in a chronological order (presenting an event in the order in which it happened). If writing a patchwork assignment, you can consider points A, B and C as the patches for exploration.

Figure 10.1 Body paragraphs from the plan in Chapter 7

The other body paragraphs can follow a paragraph structure comprising four elements: topic sentences, supporting and explorative sentences, concluding sentences and transitions.

Topic sentences. These are sentences which usually start a paragraph. They indicate to the reader the main idea explored in the paragraph. There are useful words that we can use when considering sentences: these are **theme** and **rheme** and a well-written topic sentence will include both. The theme will make clear for the reader what the paragraph is *about*, while the rheme will indicate what the author *thinks* about the theme.

Supporting and explorative sentences. These are the sentences (notice the plural – sentences) which the author uses to explore the topic (theme) and support what they think about it (rheme). Most typically, the supporting sentences are where the author will draw upon examples from a range of literature to help them explore the theme and justify the rheme. Note: a wide range of literature often helps to make the rheme more justified than simply relying on one source. Supporting sentences will often use a range of conjunctive adverbs (for example, however, in addition, similarly, in contrast, etc.) to help guide your reader through the ideas you present. (See Chapter 14 for more on this.)

Concluding sentences. These are sentences which can end your paragraphs. It may be easier to imagine that they answer the question 'So what?' They can help to help to remind the reader how what has been written contributes to the assignment – and your answer. Note that not all paragraphs require a concluding sentence.

Transitions. Transitions do what you'd expect: they move the discussion from one point to the next, and make your reader's journey more predictable and comfortable. Transitions can be presented in many ways, but some constructions you could use are backwards and forwards references (as well as ..., the following, below, next, etc.). Note that not all paragraphs will have or require a transition sentence.

EXERCISE 10.1

Read the example paragraph and identify:

- *The topic sentence (TS)*
- *Any supporting and explorative sentences (SS)*
- *The concluding sentence (CS)*
- *The transition sentence (TR)*

Communication is vital to effective osteopathic practice. Indeed, most complaints made against osteopaths result from poor communication (General Osteopathic Council, 2012). The Osteopathic Practice Standards set out 'communication and patient partnership' as the first of their four themes, and Standard A1 requires the practitioner to 'adapt communication strategies to suit the specific needs of the patient' (General Osteopathic Council, 2012:4). The specific needs of the patient will obviously change relating to different individuals but it is clear that the competent practitioner will have a range of communicative tools which can be used when interacting with patients. In order for selection of the most effective communication strategy, it is first necessary to identify any potential barriers to patient–practitioner communication. Travaline, Ruchinskas and D'Alonzo provide a checklist for the practitioner to consider potential barriers to communication, these are: 'speech ability or language articulation; foreign language spoken; dysphonia; time constraints on physician or patient; unavailability of physician or patient to meet face-to-face; illness; altered mental state; medication effects; cerebral-vascular event; psychologic or emotional distress; gender differences; racial or cultural differences; [or] other' (2005:14). Should any of these barriers be present, then it is the practitioner's duty to employ strategies aimed at overcoming them and while there is no exhaustive collection of strategies, some are outlined by Leach (2011). These strategies include considering how information can be simplified and tailored in terms of size and pace to meet a particular patient's need. As well as this, the practitioner may consider checking the patient's understanding of information by asking questions, and could draw diagrams to aid with this understanding if appropriate (Leach, 2011). This assignment now moves to the specific points of non-verbal communicative strategies.

EXERCISE 10.2

Look at one of your own paragraphs and identify these sentence types.

- *The topic sentence (TS)*
- *Any supporting and explorative sentences (SS)*
- *The concluding sentence (CS)*
- *The transition sentence (TR)*

Summary

- Each paragraph should develop one idea
- Use different types of sentences to help develop your ideas clearly
- Different sentence types can help move your reader from point to point

CHAPTER

11

Conclusions for Reflective Assignments

By the end of this chapter, you should be able to:

- Understand the purpose of conclusions
- Identify the main functional elements of conclusions
- Write effective and purposeful conclusions

Leave a lasting impression on your reader

Your conclusion is an important part of your reflective assignment, and you should take some time to plan what you should (and shouldn't) include. Your conclusion should indicate how you have answered the question, summarise the main points of the assignment, and can suggest implications for future theory or practice.

How long should a conclusion be?

Typically, like the introduction, a conclusion will occupy between 5% and 10% of an assignment's word count (see Figure 11.1). This does, however, depend on the reflective approach that you have used: sometimes you may find that you can conclude in relatively fewer words than those comprising 5% of your word count.

What should my conclusion include?

There are three functions which your conclusion can perform and while these can be presented in the order you find most logical (or they can be combined), they can be outlined as:

i. *Indicate how you have answered the question.* Here, rather than just copying the exact wording, try to demonstrate to your reader how your reflection has been used to fulfil the requirements of the question.

Conclusion	5–10%
i	
ii	
iii	

Figure 11.1 A plan of a conclusion

ii. *Summarise the main points of the assignment.* In summarising the points covered by the assignment, you have an opportunity to remind your reader of the progression of your professional practice.
iii. *Suggest implications for future theory or practice.* A conclusion is a good place to link the findings of your reflection to a wider context: you may have identified an area of not adequately covered in the literature and may want to suggest this as an area for future research.

Although the plan labels these elements separately, you don't have to write them as separate paragraphs.

EXERCISE 11.1

Read the conclusion and identify the three functions.

In sum, through reflecting on an instance from my own practice on the ward, this essay has shown the importance of upholding both the physical and relational aspects of dignity and highlighted the fact that the two cannot be separated. Through deepening my own understanding of the concepts of compassion, individual choice and fundamentals of care in upholding dignity, I have gained a clearer understanding of the importance of holistic care in upholding dignity. That is, care that is holistic in terms of relational and physical aspects, and also in terms of the entire multidisciplinary team collaborating. Having undertaken this reflection, I intend to work on three elements of my own practice: my emotional intelligence, my confidence in decision-making, and multidisciplinary working in terms of upholding dignity.

TIP

As your conclusion is there to summarise your reflection, it is important that you **don't introduce** new ideas that haven't been developed in the main body of your assignment. If you think of something else to include, consider whether it should be put in the main body of your assignment and properly developed.

EXERCISE 11.2

Look at your own conclusion and identify the three functions.

Summary

- Conclusions have three main functions: to indicate how the question has been answered, to summarise the main points of the assignment, and to suggest implications for future theory or practice
- Allocate between 5% and 10% of your word count to the conclusion

PART

2

Linking Theory to Practice

The following three chapters all deal with an aspect of reflective writing that is specific to academia: incorporating the ideas and statements of others into your work. Considering that writing reflectively is such a personal activity, it might seem peculiar that you should be asked to incorporate other authors' ideas into your work, but doing so does serve an important purpose. Your lecturers want you to understand how your actions relate to the wider conventions, legislation and conversations within your field.

TIP

For example: You reflect on an incident where a patient's privacy was compromised due to a personal conversation being held in a public space. After researching the relevant literature around privacy you understand why this should not have happened. But you also have a deeper understanding of the concept of privacy and you can apply this understanding to other incidents that may occur in the future even if they are very different in nature to the original incident you reflected on.

To put this more simply: your lecturers want to make sure that you have more than just an understanding of the key positive or negative features of an isolated incident and that you can say how you might tackle a similar situation differently next time. They want to see that you have a deeper understanding of *why* a particular course of action was or was not correct and to be able to draw on this knowledge to make the correct decisions should another related incident arise. As you learn your trade, reflection is a dual process: you are examining yourself and how you might improve, but you are also learning the theory around your subject area and building your own knowledge base. You begin to show an understanding of the link between your actions and the legislation, the previous research, and the relevant theories in your subject area. You also start to notice the differences in ideas between various authors and bodies, and learn to make judgements as to which you agree most strongly with.

You may hear this process referred to as 'linking theory to practice'. This type of writing often causes the most concern among students, as it is the most typically 'academic' in style. Following the steps outlined from here through to Chapter 14 will make the process a little less daunting.

CHAPTER

12

Theory to Practice – First Steps

By the end of this chapter you should:

- Understand the requirements of linking theory to practice
- Know how and when to include definitions within your work
- Understand the kind of evidence to draw upon and how to order it

The first steps to take when linking your theory to practice are to use sources effectively to introduce, support and explore the themes and topics you discuss. This chapter will demonstrate how you may start to do this in a number of ways. Note that you will not have to follow each of these steps for every theme you explore or paragraph you write, but successful writers often use a combination of these throughout their assignments.

TIP

Not all sections of your assignment will require you to link your practice to the theory in the ways outlined in these chapters. For example, in a Gibbs-style model, you may not be required to reference at all in the Description and Thoughts and Feelings sections, but to save discussion of literature for the Analysis. Check your guidelines carefully to see how, where (and even if!) your assignment requires you to discuss the literature around your subject.

For example:

You are writing a social work essay in which you are required to reflect on the implementation of a foster care plan for a child of parents with substance misuse issues.

Definitions you might choose to give are:

- A foster care plan

- The regulations regarding when a foster care plan should be implemented
- Substance misuse

These definitions provide your reader (and you!) with a working understanding of the issue you are reflecting on.

Providing definitions

To begin, start broad. The simplest way to begin linking theory to practice is to provide definitions of the area you will be discussing. These will very often come from governing bodies such as the Royal College of Nurses, or the World Health Organization.

Definitions are useful when you first begin writing about a subject. Places you might include them within your assignment are:

- Introductions
- Paragraphs where you introduce a subject or theme for the first time

The definitions you provide will often (but not always) be provided in quotation form.

Examples of this in practice would be:
For a condition:

The patient's diagnosis of early dementia was an important consideration when devising a care plan. The WHO (2015) defines dementia as 'a syndrome in which there is deterioration in memory, thinking, behavior and the ability to perform everyday activities' (WHO, 2015).

For a theme:

The area in which I quickly realized I was least confident in was carrying out a risk assessment alone. The RCN define a risk assessment as 'identifying the risks and hazards that might cause harm to patient/clients, visitors and staff' (RCN, 2018, p.145).

To justify the use of reflection: (Yes – you often have to provide a definition of reflection as well!)

This essay will use Gibbs' Reflective Cycle in order to reflect on an incident that occurred while on placement in a palliative care unit. Reflection is defined as 'a process of reviewing an experience of practice in order to describe, analyse, evaluate, and so inform learning about practice' (Reid, 1993).

In these examples, we would expect the paragraph to develop, delving further into the topics identified. Giving definitions in this way provides a nice way to start to link your practice to the theory around your topic. However, it is not enough to solely do this, and your lecturer will expect that you provide more than definitions. We'll now look at the first way you might do this.

'Headline' facts and figures

To show further understanding of the issue you are reflecting on you may wish to bring in related key facts and/or statistics.

For example:

Your Occupational Therapy reflection focuses on an incident where you were working with a bariatric patient. As well as providing a definition of obesity, you may also show an awareness of the issue by providing key facts and figures. Depending on the scenario, these might include:

- How many people in the world/country of study are classified as obese?
- How has this figure changed over a particular time span?
- How does this figure differ from men to women? Adults to children?

This might look something like the following:

As previously stated, the main challenge that working with Mr. Harrison presented was his weight; he presented as clinically obese with a BMI of 42. This is not an uncommon problem: latest figures from the WHO indicate that 13% of adults are categorised as obese (WHO, 2016). In the UK, this figure is higher, with 28.1% of adults now falling into the same classification. For men of Mr. Harrison's demographic the figure is yet higher, with obesity in deprived areas significantly higher among adult males (NHS, 2017).

Notice how, in this example, the writer has ordered the information in a particular way: from the broadest information (the world), to the most specific (people of a similar demographic to the patient). This isn't the only way to order data, but it can be a useful model to follow if you are wondering how to organise the facts you have found. (More on this in Chapter 14.)

TIP – A WORD OF WARNING

It can be tempting to fill the analysis section of your reflection with facts and figures of the type in the previous example. However, you must be careful to choose only the most *essential* and *relevant* data. Be selective – not all the data around the issue will be necessary. Don't fall into the trap of using facts to fill up word count!

EXERCISE 12.1

The following sentences are taken from a paragraph in a student's reflective essay. Can you put them into logical order?

1. *In light of these guidelines, it is clear that fundamental principles of care were not adhered to in this incident.*
2. *Doing this demonstrates compassion for the patient, which is one of the 6 Cs introduced by the NMC in 2012. (The others are: care, competence, communication, courage and commitment.)*
3. *Poor communication is one of the most common reasons problems occur when a healthcare worker is examining a patient with learning difficulties (MENCAP, 2016).*
4. *When the patient displayed anxiety and was clearly not responding, the nurse did not attempt to alter her communication style, or think to offer an advocate.*
5. *One way to combat communication difficulties more effectively is to utilise a range of communication methods, such as visual or written.*
6. *It also allows a healthcare professional to abide by the NMC Professional Standards Code (2015), which states that all nurses and midwives must 'prioritise people, preserve safety and promote professionalism'.*

EXERCISE 12.2

When deciding which facts and figures you do want to include, you can use both the situation, and the theme identified for guidance.

Look at the following situations and themes identified for reflection. What definitions would you have to provide? Which facts and figures would you search for in order to show an understanding of the area?

Situation for Reflection	Theme Identified
Patient's notes left on ward	Privacy
Student nurse left unattended with an aggressive patient	Assertiveness
Umbilical cord issues during birth leading to emergency C-section	Preparedness
Palliative care for lung cancer patient	Emotional Intelligence

Summary

This chapter has outlined the first steps you can take to link your theory to your practice. These are:

- Provide definitions of a key term
- Give key facts and figures
- Ask questions that will help you investigate a topic further

CHAPTER

13

Incorporating Sources into Your Reflective Writing

By the end of this chapter, you should be able to:

- Incorporate quotes correctly within your writing
- Form accurate paraphrases and incorporate them into your writing
- Provide summaries of other writers' ideas

A further skill to learn when linking theory to your practice is how to incorporate source material into your writing. Doing this correctly not only enables you to show a good understanding of your field, but ensures you do not get accused of plagiarism (when work uses ideas from other sources without referencing them).

You may incorporate source material in three ways:

1 You may **quote directly** from the source material.
2 You may **paraphrase** the source material. (Paraphrasing means to convey the same idea but using your own words.)
3 You may provide a **summary** of the source material.

In this chapter, we will look at when and how to use these techniques.

Quoting

When we quote in academic writing, we use the exact words from the source material and insert them into our own text. To demonstrate that these words come from another source, they are placed between quotation marks ('quote'). Not only do you take the exact words, but the punctuation and any special formatting such as italicisation remains the same. Every quote you use should also contain a reference to the source material, using the referencing system favoured by your institution.

While quoting is a useful way to link your practice to the wider theory, be aware that you should **use it sparingly**. Generally speaking, you should only quote in the following circumstances:

- To provide a definition, such as that given by a governing body.
- When the idea you are referencing is written using specialist, or particularly effective language.
- When referencing a primary source, such as a patient.

As a rough guide, direct quotes should make up no more than 10–20% of the references that you use. The rest should be paraphrased or summarised.

The reason for this is similar to the reason that your lecturers will ask you to link your practice to theory in reflective writing: they want to see that you really understand the ideas you are discussing. Anyone can copy and paste large chunks of relevant text; it is much harder to put the idea into your own words.

So, while bearing in mind that quoting will be the lesser used of the three techniques, here are a few tips to make sure you're doing it right.

Introducing a quote

Even though the quotes that you use are the exact words of another author, they still need to flow in the context of your writing. The following is an example of where the writer has not thought carefully enough about how this needs to happen.

A paramedic must be prepared to treat a complete range of people in a wide variety of situations. 'Paramedics are autonomous practitioners who undertake a wide range of treatment and diagnostic activities for service users across the lifespan' (College of Paramedics, 2017).

While the information in the quote is linked, the writer has done nothing to introduce it. The effect is to make the writing feel disjointed.

A couple of ways to resolve this might be:

A paramedic must be prepared to treat a complete range of people in a wide variety of situations. ***As noted by*** *the College of Paramedics (2017): 'Paramedics are autonomous practitioners who undertake a wide range of treatment and diagnostic activities for service users across the lifespan'.*

Or:

The College of Paramedics (2017) ***states that****: 'Paramedics are autonomous practitioners who undertake a wide range of treatment and diagnostic activities for service users across the lifespan'. This means that a paramedic must be prepared to treat a complete range of people in a wide range of situations.*

Introducing a quote in this way makes it easier for your reader to follow how it relates to your ideas.

Words for introducing quotations

Spend a little time and thought considering the words you use to introduce your quotations. A few examples might be:

- X claims that '...'
- As Y highlights '...'
- According to Z, privacy is defined as '...'
- X states that '...'

There are two main points to consider here:

Firstly, be aware that different 'reporting verbs' (such as 'claims', 'states') carry different connotations, and mean different things. 'Claims', for example, can have the meaning that you don't necessarily agree, while 'notes that' or 'illustrates' are much more neutral. Be aware that if you use only neutral reporting verbs, you do not signal to the reader what your view of the source material is.

Secondly, make sure you use a variety of reporting verbs to introduce the sources you discuss. It can be off-putting for your reader to come across the same word before every quotation. Further examples of these might include:

Agrees
Argues
Asserts
Claims
Comments
Compares
Declares
Demonstrates
Disagrees
Disputes
Emphasises
Illustrates
Implies
Notes
Observes
Responds
States
Suggests

Incorporating a quote

One other effective way to utilise quotation is to incorporate keywords within your sentence. This technique is useful when you don't need to quote the whole sentence, but want to use a small number of effective words direct from the source.

For example:

Service users often feel a sense of shame when arriving at a social work agency and it can take some convincing before they are ready to 'cross the agency threshold' (Davies, 1985).

So if we accept the given definition that the concept of dignity in the care of the elderly means care that 'supports and promotes, and does not undermine, a person's self-regard' then we may begin to understand how an Occupational Therapist may ensure they allow dignity to be maintained (Help The Aged, 2001).

Note that in both these examples the quotation fits grammatically within the sentence. Because you are not able to change the quotations you use in any way (even down to the punctuation!) you may have to shape your sentences around them if you choose to incorporate them in this way.

Other rules for quotations

Ellipsis points

There may be occasions when you find a quote that contains exactly what you need, but also contains some information that is not relevant to the point you are making. In this case it is acceptable to omit words from a quotation. To indicate you are doing this, use ellipsis points (three dots). For example, you may find the following quote:

'Nurses are taught to report in a narrative form providing as many details as possible about the patient or situation, while physicians communicate in an abbreviated "headline" format, focusing on key information' (Woodhall et al., 2007).

The main idea is useful to you, but you do not need the detail given in the original quote. Using ellipsis points, you may choose to incorporate the quote as follows:

Problems with communication between nurses and physicians can sometimes be put down to training. As noted by Woodhall et al. (2007) 'Nurses are taught to report in a narrative form … while physicians communicate in an abbreviated "headline" format'.

Inserting keywords

You may come across a situation where you have found the perfect quote to demonstrate your point but it is missing the keyword. In this instance you can help your reader understand your quotation by adding the keyword in square brackets into the text. For example, you may find the following quote:

'Social workers are often forced to use their own judgment, as the conflict between guidelines and practice, leaves them without a clear course of action' (Jones, 2008).

Which you could use as follows:

Jones (2008) observes that 'the conflict between guidelines and practice leaves [social workers] without a clear course of action'.

In this example, the use of the square brackets helps the writer avoid confusion that may have arisen from leaving the unclear pronoun (them) in the quote.

Adding emphasis

While as a rule, you should change nothing from the original source material when quoting, you may wish to add emphasis to a certain part of the quote that is particularly relevant to a point you have made by italicising it. If you do, it is important that you make the reader aware that the emphasis is yours. To do this, simply add the words 'My italics' or 'My emphasis' in brackets after the quotation. For example, if you were writing on the benefits of reflection you might incorporate the following quote as follows:

> *'Keeping a reflective journal has been shown to have a* significantly positive *effect on a healthcare worker's own ability to learn from their experiences' (Davies, 2011) (roman added for emphasis)*

Acknowledging errors

Very occasionally – perhaps when quoting a primary source – you will use a quote that contains a grammatical or lexical error. The temptation may be to correct this, but don't. Instead, simply acknowledge the error by adding [sic] in square brackets immediately after. This comes from the Latin 'sic erat scriptum', which means 'as it was written'.

For example:

> *I asked the patient how she was feeling and she told me 'My head been hurting now two days' [sic].*

These techniques show how you can use quotations within your academic assignments. The three main points to ask yourself when quoting are:

- Do I really need to quote (or can I paraphrase)?
- Does it flow within my writing?
- Do I need to make any extra alteration to aid understanding or shorten the quote?

Quoting is an essential tool and will almost certainly feature in every assignment you write. However, to really help your writing stand out, and to meet the requirements your lecturer is looking for, you will need to master the skill that follows: paraphrasing.

Paraphrasing

Now that you have a grasp of how to quote correctly, it's time to look at the other way of integrating sources: paraphrasing. Of the two methods of integrating source material, this is the one you should be using most. The reason? Your lecturers want to see that you have a sound understanding of the main theory around your topic. It's fairly simple to find a quote about, for example, assertiveness within the healthcare profession, and copy and paste it in to your assignment. More challenging is to take that quote and convey the same meaning in your own words. But doing this shows *understanding* – exactly the type of understanding that your instructors want to see within your discussion. What's more, it allows you to tie the ideas to your own work and mould the points you make with your own voice.

As mentioned earlier, quotes tend to be used for the following situations:

- To provide a definition, such as that given by a governing body
- When the idea you are referencing is written using specialist, or particularly effective language
- When referencing a primary source, such as a patient

Paraphrasing, then, is used for all other situations where you are using another author's idea. So how do you do it? What qualifies as a good paraphrase within academic writing?

The main features of an effective paraphrase are as follows:

- The meaning should be true to the original
- It should be distinct from the original (usually in more than one way)
- It should be grammatically correct
- It should be referenced (even if the new paraphrase is entirely your own words)

The steps to effective paraphrasing

Identify keywords

Although paraphrasing requires that we convert the original into our own words, there will naturally be some words within a sentence or paragraph that we have to keep. These might be key subject words, names or simply words where there is no real synonym.

For example:

You have found the following idea from your reading. You decide it does not require a direct quote, but you'd like to paraphrase the main idea.

> *Any consent to assessment or treatment should be gained in an informed manner and failing to do so can leave the clinician open to accusations of negligence (Gaisford, 2017).*

From this sentence, which words do you think you would not change?

Possible answers

Consent – this is the key subject word.
Negligence – as quite a specific legal term it would be hard to find an adequate synonym for this.

That means all the other words could be changed. So the next step is to find accurate synonyms (words with similar meaning; such as: 'big' and 'large').

Finding synonyms

Thesauri and, more recently, the right click button on your mouse, have a lot to answer for. With the turn of a page or the click of a mouse, you have a list of instant 'answers' that will help you in your quest to paraphrase any given sentence.

But wait! Not all synonyms are created equal. The problem with relying on the thesaurus to help you paraphrase is that it can prevent you from thinking enough about the context of the words, and the overall meaning of the sentence. To demonstrate this point by taking it to its ridiculous extreme, our original sentence could be transformed into something like this if we relied unthinkingly on a thesaurus:

> *All consent to testing or handling ought to be grown in an educated way and declining to do so can desert the doctor exposed to claims of negligence (Gaisford, 2017).*

This paraphrase doesn't provide the clear understanding your lecturers are looking for – and it isn't even grammatically correct.

This was obviously an extreme example, but it does demonstrate a serious point: it's far too easy to use a synonym that doesn't accurately convey the meaning of what you are trying to say. The word 'assessment', for example, has numerous synonyms, including: 'examination', 'calculation', 'appraisal', and 'test'. None of these quite represent the meaning of the original. Likewise, in this context the words 'in an informed manner' have a very specific meaning and it may be necessary to find a phrase that accurately represents this meaning rather than trying to paraphrase every word individually.

Therefore, to paraphrase the original sentence we might do something like the following:

Original:

Any consent to assessment or treatment should be gained in an informed manner and failing to do so can leave the clinician open to accusations of negligence (Gaisford, 2017).

Paraphrase using synonyms:

All consent to medical evaluation or intervention ought to be given with the patient's full knowledge, and not doing this could see the medical professional in danger of claims of negligence (Gaisford, 2017).

Let's check this against our original criteria for an effective paraphrase:

- **Meaning:** Yes, this seems to convey the same meaning, albeit a little more clumsily.
- **Grammatically correct:** Yes.
- **Referenced:** Yes.
- **Original:** Yes and no. Most of the words have obviously changed, but the grammatical structure is still largely the same. There is more to do to really make sure this is an original paraphrase.

Further steps for paraphrasing

Luckily for us (and your reader) there are several more techniques we can use to paraphrase.

Active to passive voice

This is a nice, simple way to change the grammatical structure of your sentence while conveying the original meaning. For example:

'The nurse cares for the patient' (active) could be changed to:

'The patient is cared for (by the nurse)' (passive).

In an active sentence, the focus is on the person doing the action. In a passive construction, the emphasis shifts to the object of the sentence (the person or thing to whom the action is being done).

In our original sentence the first clause is written in passive voice:

'consent ... should be gained'

Therefore we could change this to:

'Clinicians should gain consent ...'

With synonyms this could be changed to:

'Medical professionals should ensure they have consent ...'

Using word families

One further way to change the grammatical structure of a sentence is to change the form of a word. For example, look for the noun form of an adjective or verb, or vice versa. (If you are not confident that you can ascertain whether a word is a noun, verb, adjective, or other, a good dictionary will always give the classifications. A quick Google search will usually help you out as well.)

Looking at the original sentence, there may be opportunity to do this with the word 'accusations'.

This is a noun, but we could alter this part of the sentence in the following way:

Original:

'can leave the clinician open to ***accusations*** *of negligence' (noun)*

Paraphrase with word family:

Patients may ***accuse*** *the clinician of negligence (verb)*

Changing sentence structure

One useful thing about English is that in most sentences that contain two or more clauses, it is possible to switch the order of the clauses and retain the meaning. (A clause is sometimes referred to as a 'unit of information'. There can be anything from one or two clauses, to several within a sentence. See Appendix 3 for more information on clauses.)

In the original sentence, you could do the following:

Original:

Any consent to assessment or treatment should be gained in an informed manner and failing to do so can leave the clinician open to accusations of negligence (Gaisford, 2017).

Switched clauses:

Clinicians can be left open to accusations of negligence if they fail to gain consent to any assessment or treatment in an informed manner (Gaisford, 2017).

If you incorporate synonyms into this:

Medical professionals run the risk of being accused of negligence if they do not gain consent to any medical evaluations or interventions (Gaisford, 2017).

You may also choose to break a long sentence up into two or more parts, or turn two or three short sentences into one long one.

Use of reporting verbs

We looked at these for introducing quotes but reporting verbs can be equally as useful for introducing paraphrases, especially as they offer another way for us to structure the sentence.

For example:

Gaisford (2017) states that *patients may accuse a medical professional of negligence if the professional did not get their full permission before undertaking an evaluation or procedure beforehand.*

This last example has now moved a long way from the original. As well as using the reporting verb there is a passive–active switch, the noun *accusations* has become a verb and the clauses have been switched.

Does it pass our criteria for an effective paraphrase?

- **Meaning** – yes, this conveys the same idea as the original.
- **Grammatically correct** – yes, this reads well, and better in fact than the first attempt which only used synonyms.
- **Referenced** – yes, the reporting verb allows us to do this.
- **Original** – yes, this is now far enough removed from the original that it works as a really effective paraphrase.

Effective paraphrasing is a skill that takes some practice. However, by using different combinations of the techniques we have outlined you will soon be incorporating your source material seamlessly into your reflective assignments and satisfying your lecturers that you have a sound grasp of the subject area.

EXERCISE 13.1

Use the techniques outlined in this chapter to paraphrase the following sentences. Try and use more than one technique for each sentence.

Doctors must work on the presumption that every adult patient has the capacity to make decisions about the disclosure of his or her personal information (Harris, 2018).

Paraphrase:

....

....

....

....

....

....

....

If someone is going to have a major medical procedure, such as an operation, their consent should ideally be secured well in advance, so they have plenty of time to obtain information about the procedure and ask questions (NHS UK, 2018).

Paraphrase:

....

....

....

....

....

....

....

Summarising

Quoting and paraphrasing are both tools for taking specific facts or ideas from source material and incorporating them within your writing. However, there may be times when you do not need to include the specifics such as numbers or the details of an argument, but want to convey the essence of an idea. This is when summarising is a handy tool. The main features of summarising are:

- Gives only the main points
- Written in your own words

- As with quoting and paraphrasing, a reference is required
- Usually shorter than quotes or paraphrases

Summarising is a skill you almost certainly use regularly in everyday life. You might tell a friend briefly about the plot of a film or novel, or describe a recent weekend away. You wouldn't recite the script of a film word for word, or describe everything you ate for breakfast, but rather would try and give an overall impression. In essence, summarising within an academic assignment uses the same skills.

Consider the following example. The student has found the following paragraph from a study by Mattis and Loveridge:

The study consisted of 50 student nurses in their final year, who were observed in practice before and after taking the communication skills training. Of the five metrics assessors were looking for (greeting patients; giving their name; informing them of what treatment/checks they are going to perform; informing them of procedural difficulties; and letting them know how treatment may proceed henceforth), significant improvements were noted in all. Surprisingly, the largest difference was in the number of nurses telling a patient their name: 94% following the skills training as opposed to 48% before the training occurred. Most were already providing some form of 'commentary' as they carried out their checks and procedures, but this also showed a rise after training (78–88%) and further observations were that the commentary became more detailed in most cases in the second observation. The smallest difference was in nurses who informed patients of how a treatment plan may proceed, which went from 36% to 42%, though the low numbers for this may be due to the fact that student nurses do not always have access to this information.

The student might then summarise this in the following ways:

One study by Matiss and Loveridge (2006) found that communication training made a significant difference to nurses' practice, with communication improving across a range of areas following a short CPD session being delivered.

Student nurses do not necessarily communicate in the most effective way when first on placement. However, it has been demonstrated that even a short communication training programme can significantly improve nurses' practice (Matiss and Loveridge, 2006).

Notice how the student has taken only the key details, to give the reader the gist of the main ideas.

Summary

This chapter has covered ways to incorporate the ideas of others using three different techniques:

- Quoting – taking an author's work word for word and implementing it within your text
- Paraphrasing – putting the ideas of others into your own words
- Summarising – providing a brief 'gist' of an author's idea, without going into detail

CHAPTER

14

Writing Critically and Writing with Flow

By the end of this chapter you should be able to:

- Understand what is meant by writing critically
- Understand the difference between critical and descriptive writing
- Employ a number of techniques to help you form critical analysis of texts
- Link ideas within a paragraph
- Use a number of techniques to demonstrate criticality

The techniques for linking theory to practice that were covered in the previous chapter are useful for demonstrating a wider understanding of the issue you are discussing. However, in many reflective assignments you will be required to take this further, and demonstrate an element of *critical thinking*.

This is where the highest marks are often gained. It is also where students feel most confused. Common feedback from lecturers is that an assignment may be 'too descriptive/not critical enough', but what does that actually mean?

What is critical analysis?

You might hear the word critical and think that you are being asked to find fault with all the ideas you read. After all, that's what we mean when we say a family member or friend is 'too critical!' In an academic context though, critical analysis means the ability to break a concept down into its constituent parts, to recognise that there will often be more than one way to look at an issue, and to make a judgement, based on reasoning, about which of the ideas is most valid (Bloom, 1956). This is true in all fields of nursing, health or social work, where academics will have wide-ranging views about everything from policies to the reasons behind epidemics.

Being critical does not mean that you simply dismiss all these views, but that you understand how they are different from one another and what the merits and/or flaws of each study or argument might be. A good assignment will provide a discussion of the main ideas around a topic, while relating this back to the writer's own practice. In the following examples and exercises we'll explore what that looks like (Table 14.1).

Table 14.1 The difference between descriptive and critical writing

Descriptive writing	Critical writing
• States what an author says about a particular topic. *Jasper (2003) states that reflective practice enables healthcare students to bridge the gap between the theory they learn and the practical skills they must acquire.*	• Summarises what authors say about a topic, but also provides comment, showing why this is relevant to the assignment/the idea being discussed. *Jasper's definition of reflection – as a means by which healthcare students can bridge the gap between theory and practice – is particularly relevant, as it makes the benefits of reflection clear.*
• Gives details of a study such as results, methods etc. *Hoddinton (2013) found that 65% of student nurses do not feel confident raising issues of poor practice with their superiors.*	• Gives details of a study but also discusses how useful/relevant/appropriate these may be. *A study by Hoddinton (2013) suggests that a high percentage of student nurses (65%) lack confidence raising issues of poor practice with their superiors. However, it should be noted that this study was conducted with a very small sample size (less than 100), many of whom were in their first year of studies.*
• Presents the ideas of a number of authors *Jackson (2007) sees the NHS guidelines around palliative care as too complicated and suggested a revision. Harris (2012) feels the methods of delivery be revised to account for the high number of patients now receiving such care.*	• Synthesises the ideas and explicitly shows how these ideas are different from/similar to one another. *A number of authors see the need for changes to way palliative care is provided. Harris (2012) feels that due to the increasing number of patients receiving such care, nurses need to adapt their methods. However, Jackson (2007) feels the problem lies elsewhere, and argues that if the guidelines for care providers were simplified, a higher quality of care could be achieved.*

Integrating critical analysis into reflective writing

Critical writing starts with critical reading

When your reflective writing assignment calls for critical analysis of literature, this should be a signal that a more detailed level of reading is required. If we are looking for facts and information about a topic, it is possible that we can find these using skimming and scanning techniques, searching the text for numbers or keywords. But to critically analyse the relevant literature, you must start to probe the information further, taking a more detailed approach to your reading.

A useful method to help achieve this is to ask questions that will help you structure your critical analysis. Such questions might include:

For arguments/opinions of other authors:

- What point(s) does the author make?
- How do they back these up?
- How do these differ to the ideas of other literature on the same topic?
- What does this mean in the context of my assignment?
- Do I agree?

For studies:

- What methods were used to get the results?
- How large was the sample size?
- Did other, similar studies have different results?
- Were the methods flawed in any way?
- What does this mean in the context of my assignment?

Reading in this way is different to simply reading for understanding, and you may find that you have to return to a text several times with different questions. However, this kind of 'active' reading – where you are engaging intellectually with a text – is the first step in demonstrating the critical thinking skills your lecturers are looking for. The skill they are hoping to develop is that you learn not to take everything you read at face value, but start to question and assess opinions and data in order to form your own judgement on an issue.

A critical thinking matrix

In Chapter 5 you were introduced to some techniques which can help understand what you read and organise the literature into themes. One variation on these techniques would be a matrix, in which you have a number of columns relating to key questions you are asking of the literature. A simple version might look like the example in Table 14.2.

Table 14.2 An example critical thinking matrix

Author & date	Main idea	Methods(if applicable)	So what?
Kernisan, 2018	*Since 1998, just 4 drugs in 100 have been approved to treat Alzheimer's.*	*Data analysis*	*Treatment has proved difficult*
Bredesen, 2017	*Amyloid plaques in the brain – toxic to neutrons – stopping build up may help prevent dementia*	*MRI scan*	*One potential treatment*
UCL, 2017	*Patients with more intense pulses in neck = more chance of getting dementia*	*Study of 3,000 people*	*Again – hopes of treating earlier improved*

This kind of matrix allows you not just to separate the key ideas, but also to see at a glance the difference between these ideas and how the author arrived at them. It also provides a starting point from which you can begin to critically discuss the ideas.

Writing with flow

Read the paragraph. How well do you feel it presents the ideas?

As noted, body language played a role in helping the patient feel comfortable. A recent paper by Kackperk (2014) gives a first-hand account of how effective use of non-verbal communication enhanced her ability to provide care for her patient. Mcabe and Timmins (2013) state that paralinguistic skills are of equal importance as verbal communication skills for establishing rapport with patients. Ruesch (1961) coined the term 'therapeutic communication' to describe the interaction that occurs between a nurse and patient that has the specific goal of the patient's well-being.

You probably noticed that the writing in this example feels disjointed. In this example, the student has not spent enough time considering how the ideas connect, and the order in which the information is to be included.

So what is the 'right order'? In Chapter 12 we looked at a 'broad to specific' structure for organizing facts and figures within a paragraph.

Different types of information will call for different approaches to organisation. Some other ways might be:

- Chronologically – did one study follow/build on another? Has our understanding of the topic changed over time?
- Building blocks – does one author's view build on the work of another's?
- Extremity of views – build through authors' levels of agreement/disagreement on an issue
- Two sides of an argument – introduce the ideas of one side then the other
- A combination of the above – sometimes the information won't lend itself to just one of these organisational techniques, but will require a combination to make the information flow logically

This is not an exhaustive list of the means by which you could organise information in a paragraph. The important thing is that you are thinking carefully about all the ideas you include, and making decisions about how they relate to one another.

You could rewrite the example paragraph as follows:

As noted, body language played a role in helping the patient feel comfortable. Effective body language is a key part of 'therapeutic communication' (Reusch 1961). Indeed, Mcabe and Timmins (2013) argue that paralinguistic skills are of equal importance to verbal communication skills for establishing rapport with patients. This is backed up by a recent case study by Kacperk, (2014) who gives a first-hand account of how effective non-verbal communication enhanced her ability to care for a patient.

EXERCISE 14.1

Which of the suggested organisation methods do you think the writer has used to rewrite the paragraph above?

The keen-eyed among you will have noticed that it wasn't only the order that changed in the rewrite of the paragraph. The writer has now made use of linking words and phrases to guide the reader through the ideas. As well as helping the writing to flow, these linking words are an essential part of what makes the writing critical. Look again:

As noted, body language played a role in helping the patient feel comfortable. Effective body language is a key part of 'therapeutic communication' (Reusch, 1961). ***Indeed,*** *Mcabe and Timmins (2013) argue that paralinguistic skills are of equal importance to verbal communication skills for establishing rapport with patients.* ***This is backed up by*** *a recent case study by Kacperk (2014) who gives a first-hand account of how effective non-verbal communication enhanced her ability to care for a patient.*

They may only take up a small percentage of the paragraph, but the words used to tie the ideas together allow the writer to demonstrate her understanding of the relationship between the ideas, to change the paragraph from a list of related facts to a cohesive, flowing paragraph.

There are a number of techniques you can use to demonstrate your understanding of the theory you use in your assignment.

Transition words

These are the simple words such as 'however', 'furthermore', 'therefore' and many more that you almost certainly already use within your writing. We've already met these in Chapter 8, but it's worth highlighting the powerful work they do in showing your understanding of how ideas relate to one another.

For example:

Swansea is a beautiful city. **However**, there is a prison on the seafront.

Swansea is a beautiful city. **Therefore**, there is a prison on the seafront.

Swansea is a beautiful city **because** there is a prison on the seafront.

This example is purposefully trivial, but it does show clearly how much those simple transition words can affect the information we present.

Many students fall into the trap of using transition words they think sound 'academic' but are not quite accurate in context. (Furthermore and moreover are two of the most common offenders here.) The point is, pay careful attention to the transition words you use.

Some of the most common ways you might use transition words are shown in Table 14.3:

Table 14.3 Common transition words

Indicating contrast	Building on a point	Giving examples	Ordering events/ ideas
However	Furthermore	Specifically	Firstly,
Although	Moreover	For example,	Secondly
	Also,		Thirdly
	In addition		

Emphasising importance	Indicating results
In fact,	As a result
Of course	Consequently
Particularly	Therefore

TRANSITION WORDS – THREE HANDY TIPS

Firstly, try to build up a good 'bank' of transition words you use within your writing. It's really easy to get comfortable using just a small number, but this can cause your writing to sound repetitive.

Secondly, aim to use them frequently within your paragraphs. They act as signposts for your reader and therefore make the ideas much easier to understand.

Thirdly, use them at the beginning of sentences. This helps fluency as your reader will know what to expect after encountering a correctly positioned transition word. It also enables the rhythm of your writing to become more varied and interesting. Just as a repeated word will start to jar on your reader's ear, so will too many sentences with a similar grammatical structure. Transition words help you vary grammatical structure as well.

Interpretation sentences

A further technique for introducing critical analysis into your writing is to offer summaries and interpretations following the points you make.

For example:

Obesity has risen significantly in almost every western country over the last half century (WHO, 2015). ***This is clearly a significant problem and is one of the main reasons for the importance of health promotion in this area.***

A survey by the RCN suggests that as many as 68% of nurses report experiencing some form of verbal abuse within a twelve-month period. (RCN, 2017) ***This emphasises how serious the problem is, and why it is so important for nurses to know how to act.***

You may choose to do this after a single idea, or at the end of a group of ideas. A summary sentence such as this can also provide an effective way to transition to the following paragraph.

Tie the theory back to your practice

While it is important that you show a thorough understanding of the literature around the themes that you explore in your assignment, it is important to remember that this is a reflective piece of work first and foremost. Therefore, you should look to tie the theory back to your practice – to close the reflective loop.

In essence, you must now answer the question: So what does all this mean for me?

Ways you might choose to answer this include:

- What have you learned?
- Does the literature confirm or contradict your personal experience/findings?
- What does this mean?
- What action will you take?

In the example from Exercise 14.1, the writer might tie up the paragraph as follows:

The literature therefore confirms my decision to be aware of maintaining positive body language throughout our communication. It would seem that my body language was almost certainly a contributing factor to the patient offering positive feedback about me to my line manager.

You won't need to do this at the end of every paragraph – the writing would soon become repetitive – but you should aim to do it to round up any learning around a particular theme following your reflections.

Criticality through the levels

As you move through your programme, your critical thinking skills should develop in terms of both your own practice, and the way in which you interpret the source material you read. As such, your lecturers will be looking for more advanced levels of criticality the further into your course you go. It's not just the word counts that get longer – you will be expected to demonstrate ever more advanced analytical and evaluative skills in your assignments too. If you are new to reflective writing and this sounds intimidating, don't worry. The more you practice critical thinking, the better you get, and you may well find that you naturally advance your skills in the way your lecturers are expecting.

However, it is worth being aware of the different 'levels' of criticality that you will be expected to demonstrate. The following table presents a broad overview of the criticality expected at each level or year of study.

N.B: Your institution may be able to provide you with a more detailed version of this level overview or other specification for your particular programme. You can also find more information by researching the SEEC Level Descriptors, available from seec.org.uk (Table 14.4).

EXERCISE 14.2

Below are four examples of the same paragraph, adapted to meet the requirements of the levels shown in Table 14.4. Read through each version of the paragraph and note the differences you identify.

Level 4

Mrs. Harris told me that by taking the time to explain her results in detail and to outline what these might mean for her future treatment, I enabled her to feel more positive about her condition. Knowledge sharing with patients increases a feeling of autonomy and therefore patient satisfaction. Smith (2007) found that satisfaction rates increased following the adoption of the RCN's knowledge sharing pathway. A study by Taylor also found that patients recorded higher satisfaction rates when involved in a knowledge sharing scheme. (Taylor, 2015) Furthermore, Harrison (2011) demonstrated that for patients who were not kept informed of their treatment plans or the reasons

Table 14.4 Criticality through the levels

Level	Expectations
Level 4 *(typically the first year of an undergraduate degree programme)*	At this level you need to demonstrate an understanding of the key principles and concepts surrounding your subject and how these relate to or frame your reflection. Your lecturer is looking to see that you are able to source information in relevant places, and that you recognise there may be differences between ideas from different sources. Providing definitions, and paraphrasing as outlined in the previous two chapters will help you do this. You might also be required to demonstrate an awareness of the strengths and weaknesses of the different positions on the theme you are reflecting on. If this is the case, make sure that you state why you consider something a strength or weakness. In summary, at this level, you are expected to: • Locate information in suitable sources • Show understanding of key principles • Recognise differences between main ideas • Recognise strengths and weaknesses of main ideas
Level 5 *(typically the second year of an undergraduate degree programme)*	One key difference between this stage and Level 4, is the level of analysis that you will be required to provide. Now, rather than simply recognising that different points of view exist, you should look to provide some further analysis around these ideas and how they relate to your own reflection/development. This might mean demonstrating an awareness of why particular methods were/were not suitable for a study, or why a particular demographic or timeframe may have led to a result. You should also begin to synthesise the ideas you find, grouping together key ideas and demonstrating a sound grasp of the different arguments/principles around the topic you are discussing. In summary, at this level you are expected to demonstrate the skills from Level 4, plus: • Show an ability to analyse ideas, breaking down their strengths and weaknesses. • Begin to synthesise the ideas you discuss

(continued)

Table 14.4 (continued)

Level	Expectations
Level 6 *(typically the third year of an undergraduate degree programme)*	By now your critical thinking abilities should have become more sophisticated. Synthesis of ideas should be fluid and logical, analysis should be insightful and relevant to your reflection, and you should be providing evaluation as to which arguments/ideas are strongest and why. Your critical analysis should now tie up to a coherent whole, moving the reader logically through all the main points in order to present a sound overall argument or conclusion. In summary, at this level, you are expected to demonstrate the skills from Levels 4 and 5, plus: • Provide evaluation of the main ideas • Relate all key ideas back to your central argument • Recognise the possibility for a new approach/further research based on your findings
Level 7 *(typically postgraduate study, e.g. MA)*	At Level 7 your critical analysis takes on a new purpose. Rather than simply present the detailed understanding of the main arguments around the topic you are reflecting on, you are encouraged to use this understanding to suggest new solutions, approaches or ideas around your subject area as you are now emerging as an expert in your field. These solutions should of course, come as a result of the detailed analysis you provide in your reflection, and should be backed up and justified like all the other arguments you present. In summary, at this level you are expected to demonstrate skills from Level 4, 5 and 6, plus: • Use these critical skills to form an original approach or conclusion • Give more detailed analysis and evaluation

behind the doctors' decisions, low satisfaction rates were recorded. Therefore, it is clear that knowledge sharing increases patient satisfaction, and this is something that I will continue to incorporate in my practice.

Notes:

....

....

....

....

....

....

Level 5

Mrs. Harris told me that by taking the time to explain her results in detail and to outline what these might mean for her future treatment, I enabled her to feel more positive about her condition. Much of the literature on the subject supports this idea that knowledge sharing with patients increases a feeling of autonomy and therefore patient satisfaction. For example, a study by Smith (2007) found that the majority of patients interviewed reporting increased satisfaction rates following the adoption of the RCN's knowledge sharing pathway. In contrast to this, Jones (2014) argues that the fact these interviews were conducted in person, while the patients were still in hospital, might make them more likely to lead to positive results. However, in a later study that used online post-treatment interviews, levels of satisfaction were still reported as higher among those patients with whom information regarding their treatment was shared (Taylor, 2015). So it seems that method of interview does not affect results. Furthermore, a study using questionnaires demonstrated that patients who were not kept informed of their treatment plans or the reasons behind the doctors' decisions, low satisfaction rates were recorded Harrison (2011). Therefore, the evidence strongly suggests that knowledge sharing increases patient satisfaction, and this is something that I will continue to incorporate in my practice.

Notes:

....

....

....

....

....

....

Level 6

Mrs. Harris told me that by taking the time to explain her results in detail and to outline what these might mean for her future treatment, I enabled her to feel more positive about her condition. It seems that this scenario is not unique; much of the literature on the subject concludes that knowledge sharing with patients increases a feeling of autonomy and therefore patient satisfaction. A study which interviewed over 400 patients showed that the majority of patients reported increased satisfaction rates following the adoption of the RCN's knowledge sharing pathway. (Smith, 2007). While it could be argued that their methods were more likely to extract a positive result due to the timing of the interviews being conducted while the patients were in care and therefore vulnerable (Jones, 2014), the same findings were mirrored in a later online study, where a much less personal interview process was used. Even when patients filed their responses online, once they had returned home, their satisfaction rates were noticeably higher than the control group who had not been part of the knowledge sharing trial (Taylor, 2015). The idea that knowledge sharing increases satisfaction is further emphasised through the results of Harrision's (2011) questionnaires from Queen's Hospital, Melbourne. In this study, the majority of patients reported low satisfaction rates. Therefore, it seems there is clear correlation between these low satisfaction rates and the level of knowledge that patients had regarding their treatment. While we cannot make conclusions based solely upon the results of one small study, the evidence does seem to largely support the theory that increased patient knowledge equates to increased satisfaction. Therefore, I will continue to incorporate this approach within my practice, wherever restrictions of time and confidentiality allow.

Notes:

....

....

....

....

....

....

Level 7

Mrs. Harris told me that by taking the time to explain her results in detail and to outline what these might mean for her future treatment, I enabled her to feel more positive about her condition. It seems that this scenario is not unique; much of the literature on the subject concludes that knowledge sharing with patients increases a feeling of autonomy and therefore patient satisfaction. A study which interviewed over 400 patients showed that the majority of patients reported increased satisfaction rates following the adoption of the RCN's knowledge sharing pathway. (Smith, 2007). While it could be argued that their methods were more likely to extract a positive result due to the timing of the interviews being conducted while the patients were in care and therefore vulnerable (Jones, 2014), the same findings were mirrored in a later online study, where a much less personal interview process was used. Even when patients filed their responses online, once they had returned home, their satisfaction rates were noticeably higher than the control group who had not been part of the knowledge sharing trial (Taylor, 2015). The idea that knowledge sharing increases satisfaction is further emphasised through the results of Harrision's (2011) questionnaires from Queen's Hospital, Melbourne. In this study, the majority of patients reported low satisfaction rates. Therefore, it seems there is clear correlation between these low satisfaction rates and the level of knowledge that patients had regarding their treatment. While we cannot make conclusions based solely upon the results of one small study, the evidence does seem to largely support the theory that increased patient knowledge equates to increased satisfaction. This clearly indicates that more guidance is needed to enable healthcare practitioners to practice knowledge sharing in a variety of situations. While the guidelines set out by the RCN's Knowledge Sharing Pathway provide some general information, in Mrs. Harris' case I had to spend time researching what I could legally share. The clear benefit to patient satisfaction gained by knowledge sharing can be seen as justification for work to be done in this area.

Notes:

....

....

....

....

....

....

Summary

- You will often be required to give 'critical analysis' within your reflective writing
- Criticality is not simply being negative – it requires deep thinking about all the arguments you read
- The order you present your ideas, and the words you use to link them, can help show evidence of critical thinking
- Provide interpretations of literature where relevant
- Tie the literature back to your own practice where appropriate

CHAPTER

15

Editing and Proofreading Your Reflective Assignment

By the end of this chapter, you should be able to:

- Understand the difference between editing and proofreading
- Use techniques to successfully edit and proofread your reflective assignment
- Recognise common errors in your own reflective work and know how to fix them

Editing and proofreading – what's the difference?

As any experienced academic writer will tell you, a good essay is not written – it is rewritten. As lovely as it would be to write an entire assignment from beginning to end, the process of reflective writing – indeed any kind of writing – is almost never like this. You will almost certainly produce many drafts of an assignment before you feel happy with the result.

Two distinct processes help us shape and polish our work. *Editing* looks at the overall work, ensuring elements such as the structure, the order of ideas and the message are clear. Editing may also involve reducing (or increasing) the word count if necessary and eliminating any repetition or redundancy. *Proofreading* involves looking at your work on a 'micro' level, aiming to minimise grammar, punctuation and spelling errors.

This chapter will show how you can use each process to refine your reflective writing drafts, and finally, your finished essay.

TIP

It is often very hard to see your errors or areas for improvement when you are in the midst of writing an assignment.

Therefore, one of the most effective things you can do to help edit your work is to leave your draft for a few days before coming back to it. That way, you will approach it with 'fresh eyes'. Errors that you didn't spot before may suddenly become glaringly obvious!

Of course, this means making sure that you start your assignments early, leaving plenty of time before the deadline! (See Chapter 7 on planning your time).

Editing

We edit to make sure our work achieves its aims as effectively as it can. That might mean making changes to a whole assignment, a specific section, or even a paragraph or sentence. It might mean reordering sections, or cutting out repetition and redundancy. In essence, we edit to make sure that the ideas we are trying to communicate are clear, concise and easy to read.

With reflective writing, the aims you will be looking to achieve are usually an accurate account of the incident, experience or trigger, and related insights, a thorough analysis of the situation, perhaps relating your experience to literature, and a clear action plan for the future.

With regards to your reflective assignments during your nursing, health or social work programme, the first step of the editing process might well be adapting your notes from your reflective journal to fit the format and tone required of the assignment. This is another reason why keeping a reflective journal is such a good idea (see Chapter 4): you've already done the hardest part, which is to start.

Use the following questions to help you edit your reflective assignment. The first list gives general questions that refer to the whole document, while the lists that follow relate to the different sections you may have to write. While these do not relate to any one reflective approach in particular, you should be able to use them to help work through most of the reflective frameworks, models and cycles you will use (see Chapter 6 for an overview of different approaches to reflection).

Whole document

- Does the assignment answer the question?
- Does any section/paragraph not contribute to the overall assignment?
- Can I clearly see the purpose behind every section? Behind every paragraph?
- Does every paragraph represent a single, clearly defined idea?
- Are points supported with enough evidence where necessary?
- Are the ideas presented in a logical order?
- Are any ideas repeated?
- Are any words repeated too often?
- Are any grammatical structures repeated too often?
- Can I spot any repetition of ideas and/or redundancy within the writing?
- Is there enough to guide the reader through the ideas presented (topic sentences, transition words etc.)?
- Has adequate critical analysis been provided where required?
- Does the conclusion accurately summarise all the key points made?

Introduction

- Does the introduction clearly outline the content and order of the assignment?
- Does the introduction specify the reflective approach that will be used and why?
- Does the introduction include all required elements (such as a confidentiality statement) (see Chapter 9)?

Relating incident/experience/trigger

- Has all key information been included?
- Is the information in the correct order? (usually chronological)
- Have appropriate linking words been used to move the reader through the incident?
- Are the tenses used consistent (e.g., narrative (past) or present)?
- Is there any information that is not needed?

Analysing experience

- Does this section clearly outline the themes identified?
- If supporting literature is included, is it all relevant?
- Is all supporting literature presented in a logical order?
- Are linking words used between the points to help guide the reader through your ideas?

- Are all points from the literature distinct from one another (or do any repeat the same idea)?
- If critical analysis of literature is required in this assignment, is adequate evidence of this provided?
- Are all points from the supporting literature referenced?
- Are all points from the supporting literature adequately paraphrased or accurately quoted?

Post-reflection and conclusion

- Do you state clearly what the process of reflection has added to your understanding of your practice?
- Do you refer to all key points and themes mentioned within your assignment?
- Is any new information introduced in the conclusion? (It shouldn't be; see Chapter 11 for advice on writing conclusions.)

EXERCISE 15.1

In Chapters 8 and 9 we learned about the importance of providing an outline for your reader that allows them to predict the information that will come next. Two tools that help us do this are the introduction and the 'topic sentence' at the start of every paragraph.

Try this with your text. Read just the introduction and the first sentence or two of every paragraph.

- *Can you clearly see how the ideas are organised?*
- *Would a reader get the gist of the essay by performing the same exercise?*

This is often called 'the skim test' and it can be a good indication of whether you are providing enough signposting throughout your assignments.

EXERCISE 15.2

Find a sample of your previous reflective work (if none is available, perhaps ask a colleague or course lecturer for an example of previous work).

Read the work and consider how you might edit it, perhaps using the questions suggested in this chapter to prompt your answers.

Proofreading

Once you have edited your reflective assignment and are happy that it flows, meets all the criteria and is as clear and concise as it can be, it is time to give the work a final proofread. Now you are not looking to make structural changes, or to add or remove sections, but simply to correct any simple mistakes you may not have noticed as you were writing. These usually include errors in:

- Spelling
- Grammar
- Punctuation
- Referencing

This is not the book for a comprehensive list of all the different types of errors it is possible to make and how to correct them. However, having read many hundreds of students' reflective assignments, we do have an idea of common mistakes students are likely to make, and have listed four of the most frequent. Do you recognise any of these?

Four common errors

Easily confused words

Your word processor does a great job of underlining of some mistakes when it doesn't recognise a spelling, but you should be careful to check for mistakes that are not identified by the computer. Words such as 'advise' and 'advice', 'effect' and 'affect' are commonly confused.

For example:

I was not sure what ***affect my advise*** *would have*

Corrected:

I was not sure what ***effect my advice*** *would have*

Mixed verb forms

If you list a number of verbs (doing words) in a sentence, they should all take the same grammatical form, though students often make mistakes with this.

For example:

Following this reflection I intend to improve my communication by always asking a patient's name, always introducing myself, ***and to maintain rapport*** *throughout any treatment or procedure.*

Corrected:

Following this reflection I intend to improve my communication by always asking a patient's name, always introducing myself, ***and maintaining rapport*** *throughout any treatment or procedure.*

Unclear pronouns

Pronouns (words such as he, she, this, they) are a great tool for making your writing flow and avoiding repetition. However, when you use them, ensure it is clear what they are referring to.

For example:

Effective communication is an important way of maintaining dignity, as is consent, although the literature does not mention ***it*** *as often.*

In this sentence it is unclear what the word 'it' refers to. Possible corrections include:

Effective communication is an important way of maintaining dignity, as is consent, although the literature does not mention ***the former/latter*** *as often.*

Effective communication is an important way of maintaining dignity, as is consent, although the literature does not mention ***consent*** *as often as* ***communication.***

Incorrect use of capitals

Capital letters should be used at the start of a sentence and for proper nouns – names of people, places and organisations. They are not used for themes identified within your essay, or for other general words such as 'doctor' or 'hospital', unless you are referring to a specific person or place.

For example:

In this essay, the theme of ***Assertiveness*** *has been explored with reference to my experience working as a* ***Student Nurse.***

Corrected:

In this essay, the theme of ***assertiveness*** *has been explored with reference to my experience working as a* ***student nurse.***

As mentioned earlier, this is not an exhaustive list of the different types of errors you may find while proofreading your work, but it can be useful to look for these kinds of errors as a starting point. The more you do it, the more you will become familiar with your own common errors, and be able to easily identify them as you proofread.

TWO PROOFREADING TIPS

Read Aloud

One reason we often don't notice simple errors in our own work is that we tend to read what we think we have written, rather than what we have actually written. Reading it out loud can help solve this problem, as we have to slow down and read every word. Sometimes just hearing the words is enough to help us realise that something doesn't sound quite right.

Read a Paper Version

Our eyes take in much less when we read on a screen than when we read on paper. Therefore, to give yourself the best chance of noticing errors, print a paper copy of your final draft and work from this.

EXERCISE 15.3

Find a sample of your previous reflective work for which you have received feedback. Does the same type of error occur several times? If so, can you find out what the error is, and how to correct it? Next time you proofread your work, be sure to look out for this error.

Summary

- Proofreading and editing are separate processes, which require different approaches
- Leaving time between drafts can help you notice errors and see your work with fresh eyes
- Successful assignments often go through several drafts – see redrafting as part of the process

CHAPTER

16

Reflective Writing for Professional Development

By the end of this chapter you will:

- Understand the importance of continued reflective practice
- Be able to write reflectively for continuing professional development
- Know how to integrate practices of reflection alongside busy workloads

So far, we have looked at reflective writing from the perspective of helping you to pass your university course. You might think that once you have finished university, you can ditch the reflection and carry on with your life. Far from it. Reflection may in fact become even more important to your development after you qualify as a nursing, health or social work practitioner and begin your professional journey. If you have spent time perfecting this crucial skill throughout your studies, you will be at a great advantage as you progress through your career.

In this chapter, we'll consider how reflection can help you to become more confident in your working life and we'll give you some pointers on how to write reflectively for continuing professional development. We will also tackle some of the issues of managing to integrate the practices of reflection in your busy working life.

Why write reflectively for CPD?

So, you know why you needed to reflect when you were studying. You needed to reflect in order to pass your course and get a job! But now you have that shiny new contract in your hand do you really still need to reflect? Yes! More so now than ever.

> 'We learn by doing and realising what came of what we did' (Dewey, 1933).

While this was noted by educational theorist Dewey last century, it is pertinent to health or social work practitioners today. Reflection can help you:

- Become more confident in your own work
- Help you to improve patient or service-user care
- Rise to new challenges
- Enjoy your work more
- Gain a promotion

You'll also find that for many professional bodies, evidence of reflection is a requirement of revalidation. This is true in the cases of, for example, the General Medical Council, the Health and Care Professionals Council, and the Royal College of Nursing.

Here's what some healthcare practitioners have to say about the importance of reflective writing to them.

> *'I used to hate reflective writing when I was at uni, but now I find it really helps me gain a perspective on the things I am stressing about so that can relax when I am at home and not keep going over things that have happened at work'* (Simon, 35, Paramedic).

> *'Once, after I had witnessed a stillbirth, I was so upset and I never wanted to think about this event again. I thought about giving up on midwifery. I spoke to my mentor and she suggested that I reflect on this event in my diary. I was so pleased I did, as it enabled me to understand why I felt the way that I did, as well as understanding the importance of the care that I had been able to give the mother in this situation. Now, 15 years later, I am still a happily practising midwife'* (Ginny, 45, Senior Midwife).

EXERCISE 16.1

Discuss reflective writing practices with a colleague or mentor. What do they find are the benefits of writing? Have their perspectives on reflective writing changed over time? How do they find the time to write?

Approaching reflective writing for CPD

Throughout this book, we have focussed on approaching university reflective writing assignments. A crucial component of university assignments is that they are assessed. This means that your lecturer will have wanted to read work that was structured in a particular way and have expectations for this writing. Now, for your own continuing professional development, you may have a much more flexible approach to reflection and you may be able to experiment with a number of the approaches that we looked at in Chapter 6. You may want to try out different forms of reflection, perhaps through poetry or art if this was not something you had the opportunity to do at university. Of course, it may be that you have been tasked with writing reflectively as a means to promotion, revalidation, or to gain a professional qualification. If this is the case, you can tackle the writing in the same way that you would for a university assignment and view this as an 'assessed' piece of writing.

Frameworks for reflective writing for CPD

Apart from the approaches we looked at in Chapter 6, if you would like to have a more in-depth approach to reflection you could try exploring Johns' model of structured reflection (Johns, 2006). One of the model's key strengths is that it views reflection as a dialogue. This dialogic approach means it can be a perfect model for working with a mentor or supervisor in practice. Another perspective on reflection that will be worth exploring in detail is Schön's differentiation between *reflection-in-action* and *reflection-on-action* (Schön, 1983). In particular, reflecting 'in-action' means that as a practitioner, you can get used to reflecting on a situation while it is ongoing with a view to helping you improve your practice at that time rather than in preparation for similar future events. Try varying the approaches you use when you are writing as they may give you different insights. After some time, you'll find that reflection comes naturally and you may not even need to use one of the frameworks, models or cycles.

Using a template to record reflections

Check to see whether your relevant professional body has a form that can be used or adapted as a guide for recording your written reflections. Some examples of these are:

- A critical reflection log for child and family care (for newly qualified social workers – this document was produced by Skills for Care in partnership with the London Borough of Merton, but can be adapted for your own use). Available at https://www.skillsforcare.org.uk/Documents/Learning-and-development/ASYE-child-and-family/Critical-reflection-log-child-and-family-template.doc (accessed 23 July, 2019).

- The Chartered Society of Physiotherapists' online e Portfolio for members to log CPD including reflections. https://www.csp.org.uk/news/2017-03-06-free-cpd-resources-csp-members (accessed 23 July, 2019).
- The reflective accounts form produced by the Nursing and Midwifery Council. This is mandatory for use with five reflective accounts for revalidation. Available at: revalidation.nmc.org.uk/download-resources/forms-and-templates (accessed 23 July, 2019).

These are just a few examples of support for reflection available on the web, but there are loads more out there so see what you can find!

Finding time to write

Finding the time to write may seem like an added worry to your already overly stressful life and you might just want to put your feet up and enjoy a glass of wine after a busy working day. However, finding the time to reflect on your practice can actually help you to de-stress in the long run.

Here's what one healthcare professional has to say about finding the time for reflective writing.

> *'I usually write in my work diary before I go home at the end of every week. This only takes me five minutes each time, but it means that when I come to do my annual review, I have plenty to write about without having to spend much time trying to remember what happened'* (Fin, 29, Mental Health Nurse).

If you follow the tips in Chapter 4 and write little and often, you will have a wide selection of events to choose from when you come to write a reflective piece for CPD, appraisal or revalidation. For this, it is far better to focus on one or two events that perhaps follow a particular theme than to reflect superficially on a large number of events.

TIP – SHARE YOUR WRITING WITH OTHERS

Try practising 'social writing'. You may need to share your writing with your supervisor or mentor as part of a formal process, but what about getting together with peers to share and talk about your writing? You can even make the writing process itself a social event. Set up a "Reflective writing for CPD" group (even if you don't have the time to meet regularly in person, you can be motivated by the fact that others are writing too).

EXERCISE 16.2

Use the space on the right to plan your writing sessions for the week ahead. If you know you have a particularly difficult day at work coming up, you might want to plan the session to reflect on this.

Day	Plans for the day and writing times if any
Monday	
Tuesday	
Wednesday	
Thursday	
Friday	
Saturday	
Sunday	

EXERCISE 16.3

Use the prompts for a writing exercise in a reflective writing group. Everyone can try writing for five minutes under each of the headings. You could also use these prompts for writing individually to reflect on your current practice.

Writing session 1.

One thing that went well this week
How I felt about this
One thing that could have gone better
How I felt about this
What I'd like to know more about as a result
Whom I can ask or where I can look to find out more
Before the next writing session, read up on whatever you noted that you wanted to find out more about.

Writing session 2.

How I feel now about the events I wrote about last week
What I found out about through reading/talking to others
What I would like to change as a result of my reflections
What I would still like to find out more about
You can share what you have written or take it away to develop on your own.

Summary

- Reflective writing can help you formally or informally with CPD and career progression
- Reflective writing is mandatory in many fields
- Establishing the habit of writing little and often will help you in your reflective practice
- Seeing writing as a dialogue can help you in your reflection

APPENDIX

1

Examples of Different Types of Reflective Writing

This appendix is comprised of three example assignments, each of which uses a different reflective framework.

Assignment 1

Critically discuss one key aspect of the NMC Code of Practice and relate this to your professional development through reflecting on your experiences on the ward.

Dignity is a key concept in nursing and integral to the Nursing and Midwifery Code of Practice. The NMC states that in prioritising people, its members should 'treat people as individuals and uphold their dignity' (NMC, 2018).

The complexity of the concept is reflected in the many different perspectives on dignity. The Royal College of Nursing defines dignity as being 'concerned with how people feel, think and behave in relation to the worth or value of themselves and others. To treat someone with dignity is to treat them as being of worth, in a way that is respectful of them as valued individuals' (RCN, 2008), thus alluding to both the physical and relational aspects of dignity. Research has suggested that while elderly patients and their relatives place more importance on the physical aspects of care in upholding dignity, healthcare professionals often place more value on the relational aspects (Cairns et al., 2013). There are many competing demands on a nurse's time, and the nurse needs to ensure that both physical and relational dignity remain at the forefront of care, even when under time and other pressures.[1]

---

1 In order to critically discuss dignity, the student has highlighted that there are different definitions of dignity and also considered the fact that service users and nurses may value different aspects of dignity. He then sets out which approach is used in the essay and highlights exactly which aspects of dignity as recognised in the NMC are explored.

This essay discusses the importance of holistic care in upholding dignity and recognises that the physical and the relational elements of dignity cannot be separated. It does this by means of reflecting on an event from my placement on a geriatric ward caring for a 92-year-old male diabetic amputee. I consider how my understanding of the concept of dignity has been deepened through this reflection. Specifically, I consider dignity as defined under the NMC code of conduct. The following three elements of upholding dignity are explored: treating patients with compassion, recognising diversity and individual choice, and delivering the fundamentals of care. From this perspective, I identify emotional intelligence, confidence and decision-making abilities as key areas for my own personal development in order to provide holistic care that upholds dignity.[2]

Reflection is a key tool in helping trainee nurses to improve their practice and skills but reflective techniques need to be used effectively as a strategy for learning (Jasper, 2003). I use the *What? So what? Now what?* reflection framework developed by Driscoll (2007), as this allows a clear means of structuring my essay with a number of trigger questions to guide the reflection process.[3]

In accordance with the NMC (2018), all names have been replaced with pseudonyms.[4]

What?[5]

I chose to focus on this event because I felt that my supervisor, 'Maggie', had been able to treat the elderly gentleman with dignity despite the time constraints we were under. I was unsure of my own role in the event or if I would have been able to act as Maggie did had I been solely responsible for the patient's care. I wanted to understand which of the actions Maggie had

---

2 This essay has two levels of reflection. Firstly dignity (relational and physical) is the umbrella theme. Compassion, individual choice and fundamentals of care are the three subthemes of the umbrella theme of dignity. In the second level of reflection, the student has identified three areas of development for his own practice that will help him to uphold dignity – these are emotional intelligence, decision-making, and confidence. Depending on the level of qualification you are working towards, you may only need one level of reflection (e.g. dignity and the three subthemes).

3 The student makes it clear in the introduction which approach to reflection is used and why.

4 The student highlights observed professional standards on anonymity. You should check your relevant professional body to see how you need to anonymise service user data and make it clear that you have observed any standards.

5 The student doesn't write in detail about everything that happened (for example, which medicines were administered) as this is not the focus of the reflection. Keeping this section short allows the student to save precious word count for the more critical 'So What?' and 'Now What?' sections.

taken made such a positive impression on me, why this was, and what I could learn for my own practice in caring for elderly patients.

This was my first week on the geriatric ward and we were working to a tight timescale to administer medicines to patients. My supervisor and I entered the ward. The first patient we saw was John, an amputee of 92 with severe type two diabetes. John is hard of hearing. He does have a hearing aid, but often turns it off as he says the ward is too noisy. John is able to lip-read well.

The first thing I noticed on approaching John's bedside was the stench – he had obviously soiled his bedclothes and this made me recoil inwardly. Maggie closed the curtains around the bed and then said cheerily "afternoon John, how are you today?" John did not reply. Then Maggie moved in front of John so he could see her mouth and smiled. She said in a quiet voice, 'good morning, John. How are you today? We'll just get these sheets changed and then check your medicines, ok?'. As she did so, she touched John's arm and he smiled back at her and nodded.

After changing the bedclothes and giving John a bed bath with the help of two nursing auxiliaries, Maggie and I checked John's notes and administered his medicines. I asked John if he was hungry and wanted to eat his sandwich. Then I remembered that I had read in John's notes that he had a kosher diet so I picked up the plate with the untouched ham sandwich and asked John if he would prefer something different. John asked for a cheese sandwich. I stood in front of John so he could see my lips and spoke quietly as Maggie had done.

So what?[7]

Through considering my own behaviour and the behaviour of others, I reflect on the relational and the physical aspects of upholding dignity that went well and those that could have been improved. Through focussing on three aspects of dignity, I consider how it can be upheld through a holistic approach to care and that the physical and relational are necessarily intertwined. The three elements of dignity focussed on are: treating people with compassion, recognising diversity, and individual choice, and finally, delivering the fundamentals of care. I consider areas of my own practice as well as qualities that I need to develop in order to effectively deliver these elements of care.

Treating people with kindness, respect, and compassion is a key element of upholding dignity (NMC, 2018), which Maggie demonstrated throughout this event. While kindness and respect are clear to me, compassion was a more difficult concept to translate into my practice and one I wanted to explore in more detail. Indeed, it has been widely reported that while compassion is a quality of nursing highly valued by patients, nurses can often have difficulties ascertaining which aspects of care convey compassion (von Dietze & Orb, 2001). John was hard of hearing and Maggie needed to talk to him about a sensitive issue. That is, she wanted to reassure him that we would change his bedding and that this was not a problem. She did this quietly in a way he could understand rather than raising her voice or forcing him to turn on his hearing aid. Her quiet tone, as well as the act of closing the curtain around the bed when we first entered, meant that Maggie was able to maintain John's privacy. While changing John's bedding and bathing him attends to a 'physical' aspect of John's care (I return to this in the next section of the essay) the physical and the relational could not be separated. To me, Maggie's actions here embody compassionate nursing. Reflecting on Maggie's actions has allowed me a deeper appreciation of how everything we do is linked to compassion. Indeed, this idea is backed up by von Dietze and Orb who state that 'though compassion is inextricably linked with action: listening, feeding, clothing ... it is not such actions in or of themselves which are compassionate, but *the way in which they are carried out*, the attitude and approach' that is important (von Dietze & Orb, 2001, p. 171).

I had read of the importance of the nurse becoming emotionally resilient and intelligent in order to be able to perform the actions required for caring in a compassionate way without being negatively affected (for example van Zyl & Noonan, 2018; Grant & Kinman, 2015). The importance of developing my 'emotional skillset' became clearer to me as I reflected on the difference between my own and Maggie's reactions when we first entered the ward. Maggie had come across as very 'matter of fact' and friendly which seemed to make John comfortable. Maggie even touched John's arm in a reassuring way when she was talking to him. I, on the other hand, felt disgusted by the smell which meant I did not want to go near John and also ashamed at my own reaction. As noted by van Zyl and Noonan (2018, p. 1192), 'when delivering compassionate care, the expected emotional state may not always spontaneously arise, risking a dissonance between authentic and displayed emotion'. While I do not know exactly how Maggie felt, she was able to remain outwardly calm when faced with an unpleasant situation. This has made me realise that in my own practice I can sometimes appear to lack compassion through, for example, not displaying a friendly demeanour or offering a reassuring touch when it would be welcomed. It is important for the nurse to acknowledge times when emotions and intent are not in harmony but to ensure these emotions do not interfere with the ability to provide compassionate care in upholding dignity or negatively affect a nurse's own state of mind (van Zyl & Noonan, 2018). Essential in a nurse's development are therefore the qualities of emotional intelligence and emotional resilience.

A second major theme emerging from my reflection on this event is the importance of recognising diversity and respecting individual choice (as stipulated in the NMC Code (2018)). While I have always prided myself on respecting the diverse needs and choices of patients, reflecting on this episode made me aware of how it is not only my own behaviour that I may need to be mindful of, but also that of others. At the time, I felt proud that I had noticed John's individual dietary requirements; indeed, my supervisor commended me on this afterwards. However, it was far from satisfactory that the member of staff who had given him his lunch previously had not paid better attention to his individual needs. I now realise that either Maggie or I should have pursued this. Even if it had been a one-off oversight, it should have been brought to the attention of whomever had made the mistake, if not to a superior, to ensure it did not happen again. This highlights the importance of an interdisciplinary approach where the emphasis is on all healthcare workers working collaboratively with the common aim of caring for a patient (Ndoro, 2014). I cannot uphold dignity on my own – my role as part of a multidisciplinary team is vital.

Although John was 'able' to eat his meal physically, and it is true that nurses should be ensure that patients are able to eat (Bloomfield & Pegram, 2012) there was actually a relational need in respecting individual choice that overrode this physical 'ability' and prevented John from eating his sandwich. This was another example demonstrating how the physical and relational are inextricably linked and that care needs to be provided holistically without nurses making assumptions. One key role of the nurse is in monitoring food intake (Bloomfield & Pegram, 2012), and in this case, the monitoring was not only physical. I am proud that I noticed that John required a kosher diet and should not have been given a ham sandwich. I am satisfied that the care delivered to John by myself and my supervisor was of a satisfactory standard and have noticed that I am generally observant in recognising individual differences. However, I am troubled that this fact was not noticed by the staff distributing food, and though I am sure it would have been remedied at once had John requested different food, the member of staff should have read his notes properly while John was sleeping. John was comfortable in asking for a different sandwich when I asked him. If I had not noticed his dietary requirements, he may have thought he had to wait until the food trolley came around again. Though the nurse's role has changed in recent years in relation to mealtimes, with healthcare workers and assistants playing more of a role in assisting patients, it is vital that the nurse communicate with other healthcare workers about all aspects of patient nutrition (Green, 2011; Bloomfield & Pegram, 2012).

The third aspect[6] of upholding dignity discussed here is delivering the fundamentals of care effectively. That is, ensuring those receiving care experience clean and hygienic conditions and that nutrition, hydration and bladder care is attended to (RCN, 2018). Maggie called the nursing auxiliary and we changed John's bed sheets immediately when she saw that this needed to be addressed. I felt confused about whether to change the bedclothes first or give John his medicine. I feel less confused now as having considered how my supervisor acted, I would know what to do next time. As noted by Lundberg, sharing stories with, and observing more experienced nurses can be a key way of trainee nurses improving their confidence (Lundberg, 2012). In this instance, I was able to observe how the appropriate care was given without undue delay as advocated by the NMC (2018). At the time I felt that we had done something wrong in not quickly administering the medicines as this is what we had been 'tasked' with doing.

I realise now that having the confidence to make decisions about the priority of tasks can also be crucial to delivering the fundamentals of care. The most urgent task in this case in terms of providing care with dignity or physical care was to deal with the soiled bedsheets. The administration of John's medicine was routine rather than urgent and could wait until we had ensured conditions were hygienic (that is 'in making sure those receiving care are kept in clean conditions and given care without undue delay' (NMC, 2018)). Maggie first asked me what I felt about my own role in the event. When I said that I had wanted to give the medicines first she stated this was something that we should not have done, but that the ability to judge this would come with confidence and experience. I agree with Maggie that my confidence in my own abilities to make decisions in all areas of my nursing practice will grow with experience and through further targeted training (Lundberg, 2012; Thompson & Dowding, 2002).

Another aspect relating to the fundamentals of care and ultimately my own confidence in delivering these is the nutritional care of the patient. While it was right to change the food that the patient had been given in an individual instance, it would have been better to have pursued this and to have checked that his dietary requirements were being met in general, especially as this was a diabetic patient. As noted by Bloomfield and Pegram (2012), nurses play an essential role in ensuring patients' nutritional needs

---

6 The themes are signposted with first, second and third to help guide the reader through the essay.

are being met. I have realised that part of my transition from being a novice to an expert nurse is having the confidence in my own decisions (Lundberg, 2008), and that I generally defer to what I perceive to be the authority of tasks, lists and routines to avoid taking responsibility for my decisions.

Now what?[7]

There are a number of ways I will change my future practice as a result of the reflections here. Firstly,[8] in order to treat patients with compassion, I will think not just about the actions I perform to care for service users but the *way* in which I perform these actions. This means noticing individual circumstances and adjusting my behaviour accordingly. In particular, I need to develop my emotional intelligence to ensure that where my internal feelings are at odds with my intentions, I am still able to deliver compassionate care. For example, I may need to be more creative in my communication with patients through involving deliberate reassuring touch where appropriate. If I do not take the opportunity to work on my emotional intelligence, I risk not placing compassion at the core of my nursing practice and would risk acting without thinking about 'how' I act.

The second way in which I will change my practice is to ensure that as well as treating patients as individuals in my own practice and recognising their individual choices, I will also pay attention to how others I am working with are able to respect the individual and their choices. I need to recognise that in working together as a multidisciplinary team, it is not satisfactory to ignore the actions of others and merely concentrate on my own practice. In future, if there is something that I am troubled about in the way a patient has been cared for, I will voice my concerns through the relevant channels to ensure that satisfactory care is given; if I do not do this, I may indirectly put service users at risk. I need to put the needs of the service user above the professional pride of a colleague who is not performing adequately.

Finally, though not any less important, I need to have the confidence to act on my own instincts and make decisions independently according to the circumstances rather than being so rigid and practising 'cookbook

7 In the *Now what?* section, the student follows up with an action point for each of the themes that were mentioned in the *So what?* section. This section broadens out from the events which the student was reflecting on to think about what it means for his practice in general.

8 There are three action points here which follow the three themes in the *So what?* section.

nursing' (DiCenso, Cullum, & Ciliska, 1998). If I do not develop confidence in my ability to judge which aspects of care need to be prioritised, I risk not only failing to deliver the fundamentals of care, but will also limit my own career progression if I need to check each decision.

The reflective process has opened a number of learning opportunities I wish to pursue. I plan to research the relational aspects of upholding dignity and need to ensure I work on my own emotional resilience. In particular, I am interested in discovering more about the perspectives of elderly patients and will conduct additional literature searches on the topic of compassion in elderly care. On a day-to-day basis in my own work, identifying patient perspectives and ensuring their needs are being met will involve talking to patients on the ward and their relatives about personal choices and asking them if their needs are being met. A final aspect of my own learning that I need to work on is confidence in my own decision-making abilities. With regard to this, I am confident that pursuing the other identified needs will in turn lead to increased confidence, but specific strategies that I can use to work on building my confidence include role playing, engaging with a peer mentor scheme, sharing my stories with peers and journaling (Lundberg, 2012).

Through undertaking reflection and the learning I intend to do, if a similar situation were to happen again, I would think about the *way* I take actions in order to be compassionate, confident enough to challenge inadequate care that others may be providing, and trust my own instincts as to what to prioritise in terms of administering care swiftly rather the adhering strictly to a plan. In order to see whether I have been able to successfully integrate the reflections on my practice in to the way I deal with patients and other healthcare professionals, I will continue to reflect on my practice in my weekly journal and I will speak to my mentor to ask for feedback on issues such as the *way* I deliver care and my confidence in decision-making.

In sum, through reflecting on an instance from my own practice on the ward, this essay has shown the importance of upholding both the physical and relational aspects of dignity and highlighted the fact that the two cannot be separated. Through deepening my own understanding of the concepts of compassion, individual choice, and fundamentals of care in upholding dignity, I have gained a clearer understanding of the importance of holistic care in upholding dignity. That is, care that is holistic in terms of relational and physical aspects, and also in terms of the entire multidisciplinary team collaborating. Having undertaken this reflection, I intend to work on three elements of my own practice: my emotional intelligence, my confidence in decision-making, and multidisciplinary working in terms of upholding dignity.[9]

References[10]

Bloomfield, J., & Pegram, A. Improving nutrition and hydration in hospital: the nurse's responsibility.

Cairns, D., Williams, V., Victor, C., Richards, S., Le May, A., Martin, W., & Oliver, D. (2013). The meaning and importance of dignified care: findings from a survey of health and social care professionals. *BMC geriatrics, 13*, 28. doi:10.1186/1471-2318-13-28

DiCenso, A., Cullum, N., & Ciliska, D. (1998). Implementing evidence-based nursing: some misconceptions. *Evidence Based Nursing, 1*(2), 38.

Driscoll, J. R. G. N. *Practising clinical supervision: a reflective approach for healthcare professionals* (2nd ed.).

Jasper, M. (2003). *Beginning reflective practice* (2nd ed.). Andover: Cengage Learning.

Lundberg, K. M. (2008). Promoting Self-confidence in Clinical Nursing Students. *Nurse Educator, 33*(2).

Ndoro, S. (2014). Effective multidisciplinary working: the key to high-quality care. *British Journal of Nursing, 23*(13), 724-727. doi:10.12968/bjon.2014.23.13.724

Nursing and Midwifery Council (2018). The Code: Professional standards of practice and behaviour for nurses, midwives and nursing associates.

RCN definition of dignity (2008) available at: https://www.rcn.org.uk/professional-development/publications/pub-003298 (accessed 23/11/2018).

van Zyl, A. B., & Noonan, I. The Trojan War inside nursing: an exploration of compassion, emotional labour, coping and reflection. (0966-0461 (Print)).

von Dietze, E., & Orb, A. (2001). Compassionate care: a moral dimension of nursing*. *Nursing Inquiry, 7*(3), 166-174. doi:10.1046/j.1440-1800.2000.00065.x

---

9 Though there is not a specific recognised word count recommended for each framework or model (unless suggested by your lecturer), you need to ensure that the sections where the most critical analysis is required have the highest word count. In the Driscoll model, these sections are the *So what? and the Now what?* Sections. This student has divided up the word count roughly as follows:

Introduction: 5–10%
What?: 10%
So what?: 20%
Now what?: 10%
Conclusion: 5–10%

Note that in this specific essay, the conclusion is actually shorter than the introduction, but it does everything that is required of a conclusion. That is, it shows how the student has answered the question and pulls out the key themes that the reader should be left with.

10 This essay uses the APA 6th style of referencing. Check which style is required by your institution. You should only include the references that you have cited (either directly or in a paraphrase) in your text and not everything you have read.

Assignment 2

You are required to write a patchwork text assignment which illustrates and analyses your personal and professional development

Tim Walker, the Chief Executive of the General Osteopathic Council, has recently written about the importance of continuing professional development (CPD) for practitioners. Part of this CPD is the necessity to reflect on clinical experiences so that the practitioner and student practitioner can evaluate their practice and identify areas of strength as well as those for improvement.[1] Indeed, the perceived value of reflection and its link to improved patient outcomes has been gaining increasing attention globally (Spadaccini & Esteves, 2014; Lewis, Farber, Chen, & Peska, 2015). This assignment will draw on different stimuli in order to develop my knowledge and competence as a student practitioner, analyse the care I have provided, and consider development needs to extend the scope of my skills. These entries will form patches, which are then explored and represent assignment segments in themselves. The juxtaposition of different stimuli as a basis for evidencing learning development was first proposed by Richard Winter in an article he wrote for *The Guardian* in 2003; and while he suggested that this 'patchwork' form of assessment would benefit students of all disciplines, those studying healthcare programmes have generally found this form of arrangement conducive to reflective practice and facilitating learning (Smith & Winter, 2003).[2] I present three patches to illustrate and analyse my personal and professional development during my second year at university: the first is an entry from my diary written on my first day in clinic, the second is another diary entry written during the mid-winter break, and the third is an image that helped to stimulate my interest in learning.[3] In presenting these patches, I identify three themes for my personal and professional development: assertiveness, communication, and knowledge of chronic low back pain.[4]

1 This introductory sentence demonstrates the relevance of the topic.

2 This part contextualises the assignment.

3 This sentence guides the reader through the remainder of the assignment to eliminate surprises.

4 Although no reflective framework is specified in the introduction (as one isn't explicitly followed), the patches tend to follow Driscoll's reflective prompts.

Patch one: entry from my diary from my first day in clinic

> Had my first day in clinic today! It seems like I've been building up to it for ages ... I was really nervous at first and worried that my lack of experience would be obvious and that the patients would think that I was incompetent but Jenny said at the start of the day to remember that we're on a journey and that we never stop learning. That really helped me realise that I wasn't expected to know everything from day one.
>
> I saw a few patients and shadowed Jenny, who explained what she was doing when manipulating the first patient's shoulder – I think that this was for my benefit but the patient also seemed really interested in finding out more about what was going on.
>
> We went for a sandwich and a coffee over lunch and Jenny explained the range of treatments which the patient whose shoulder she manipulated had received and speculated on the cause behind the soreness experienced. I'm glad she did this as I was meaning to ask her about the kinds of treatments which could be provided for this patient and which order they should be done in.

As the title suggests, this entry was written on the evening of my first day in clinical placement. Reading it now, I am able to still vividly remember the feelings I had on the first morning, and particularly my worries about appearing incompetent. There is one main issue which I am able to identify from this entry which helps to chart my personal and professional development: my own assertiveness.

Assertiveness is something that I feel I have always lacked. The youngest of my siblings, I probably became accustomed with not being listened to and this seems to have translated into my professional practice. I am not unique in this way, as non-assertive behaviours are suggested to be encouraged from childhood: it is considered good behaviour to be quiet and obedient (Bolton, 1986 in IpAC, n.d.). More specifically, it is not unusual for newly-qualified healthcare practitioners to face challenges in relation to assertiveness (Flying Start NHS, 2018) but clearly such challenges need to be overcome, as this characteristic is a 'crucial' skill in effective healthcare delivery (Harley, 2014).

My challenges related at that time to recognising my position in the educational journey and based on this recognition, to be comfortable to ask questions of Jenny when they arose. According to Morrissey and Callaghan (2011), assertive communicators clearly express their needs, wants and opinions; and as such, my failure to clearly communicate my needs at that time by asking questions appears to be linked to my lack of assertiveness. As it happens, although I now recognise that I *did have* questions, I think that I would not have remembered them, or thought about them had Jenny not joined me for lunch. Indeed, if she had not joined me, I wonder whether I would ever have answered them. In this way, I was lucky that she answered my questions without being asked.

I consider my unwillingness to ask questions as one *symptom* of my lack of assertiveness. In this way, I strive to be aware of other symptoms of this and to recognise them if and when they occur. Under-assertive individuals tend to exhibit other characteristics; for example, they are often self-effacing, avoiding confrontation and experiencing difficulty in decision-making (Morrissey & Callaghan, 2011). It is clear that in order to be a more effective practitioner, being assertive is a part of my practice which I should seek to develop. According to Balzar-Riley, developing assertiveness will result in goals being achieved and as a result of identifying this development need, I have researched techniques for developing this trait as this will benefit both patients and practitioners (Hodgetts, 2011).

Patch two: entry from my diary from the mid-winter break

It's Boxing Day – and here I am, writing in my diary! My grandma and granddad came over for lunch today and we had a really nice piece of salmon with more of the Christmas trimmings left over from yesterday. I'm not sure how much I've eaten but it feels like some kind of record!

After eating, we did what we always do: sat around the fire and argued about which game to play before deciding on charades. Dad unsurprisingly fell asleep, so me and mum made up one team and grandma and granddad were the other. It was so much fun – grandma and granddad won by a mile but I was struck by how full of life they are – and how much fun we were all having. Grandma and granddad have some kind of telepathic bond – I couldn't believe how quickly they were getting answers. Grandma just raised an eyebrow and granddad shouted 'gone with the wind': unbelievably the right answer. They have such a close bond and it's lovely spending time with them.

This entry into my diary was made on Boxing Day – at a time when studying was not at the forefront of my mind – but I had got into the habit of writing something down every day and after I had finished writing I started thinking about what I had written and how it links with my personal and professional development. Most striking from my entry was the close bond between my grandparents and their almost telepathic ability to communicate which was evident during the non-speaking game, charades. Although this demonstration of effective communication was not from an osteopathic experience, I have since reflected on what it means to communicate and how to do it effectively in a clinical setting.[5]

Communication is vital to effective osteopathic practice.[6] Indeed, most complaints made against osteopaths result from poor communication (General Osteopathic Council, 2012). The Osteopathic Practice Standards set out 'communication and patient partnership' as the first of their four themes, and Standard A1 requires the practitioner to 'adapt communication strategies to suit the specific needs of the patient' (General Osteopathic Council, 2012, p. 4). The specific needs of the patient will obviously change relating to different individuals but it is clear that the competent practitioner will have a range of communicative tools which can be used when interacting with patients. In order for selection of the most effective communication strategy, it is first necessary to identify any potential barriers to patient-practitioner communication. Travaline, Ruchinskas and D'Alonzo provide a checklist for the practitioner to consider potential barriers to communication, these are: 'speech ability or language articulation; foreign language spoken; dysphonia; time constraints on physician or patient; unavailability of physician or patient to meet face-to-face; illness; altered mental state; medication effects; cerebral-vascular event; psychologic or emotional distress; gender differences; racial or cultural differences; [or] other' (2005, p. 14). Should any of these barriers be present, then it is the practitioner's duty to employ strategies aimed at overcoming them and while there is no exhaustive collection of strategies, some are outlined by Leach (2011). These strategies include considering how information can be simplified and tailored in terms of size and pace to meet a particular patient's need. As well as this, the practitioner may consider checking the patient's understanding of information by asking questions, and could draw diagrams to aid with this understanding if appropriate (Leach, 2011).[7]

Given the range of potential barriers to effective communication and the necessity for the practitioner to overcome them, it is of utmost importance for osteopathic practitioners to identify the unique needs of each of their patients. I have always felt that I have a good manner in practice but have not considered how I can adapt communicative strategies to meet the needs of specific individuals. Instead, I may have subconsciously been employing a 'one-size-fits-all' approach which does not adequately treat patients as individuals. Failing to do this would

5 This paragraph performs the 'What?' function of reflection.

6 Topic sentence demonstrating theme and rheme.

7 This paragraph performs the 'So what?' function of reflection.

constitute a dereliction of duty; for this reason, I have identified communicative strategies as an area I wish to develop while I am in the clinical setting. I intend to attend the patient-physician partnership conference next summer which is inviting speakers on the theme of effective communication.[8]

Patch three: a striking image

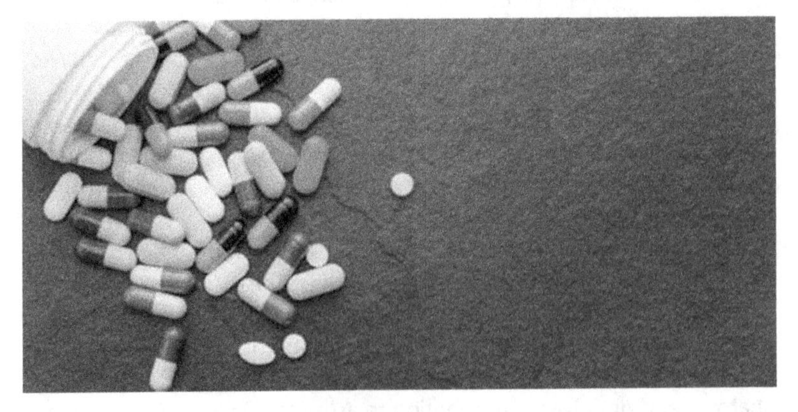

Getty Images/iStockphoto, used with permission

This patch draws on an advertising image for painkillers reported in a newspaper. Upon reading the article, it dawned on me how many of our patients at clinic suffer with chronic low back pain. This is a condition which can be complex to treat and can be associated with other determinants of health; however, like communicative strategies in the previous patch, my knowledge relating to these is not as rich as I would like. For this reason, I have identified this specific complaint as an area which would be prudent for me to research and contribute to my personal and professional development. In their Osteopathic Practice Standards, the General Osteopathic Council identify knowledge, skills and performance as their second core theme governing validation. Specifically, Standard B2 requires that the practitioner has 'sufficient knowledge and skills to support' practice as well as 'sufficient knowledge of psychology and social determinants of health' (General Osteopathic Council, 2012, p. 9).

Chronic non-specific low back pain is one of the leading causes of functional disability and as such, is a common complaint of patients (Cohen & Hooten, 2017). Because of its prominence, studies into the phenomenon continue to receive significant academic interest (Hoy et al.,

8 This paragraph performs the 'Now what?' function of reflection.

2014; Orrock & Myers, 2013); however, there is not yet consensus on its causes nor its most effective treatments. The pathogenesis of the phenomenon is likely to be derived from a combination of psychosocial, physiological and neurological factors – with different studies finding distinct links between chronic low back pain and its causes or correlations. Psychosocial factors explored include subjects as diverse as depression and cigarette smoking, although there is disparity in the findings of such studies. For example, Balague, Mannion, and Cedraschi (2011) suggest a slight association between non-specific low back pain and smoking status while earlier studies have suggested more significant links (for example Alkherayf & Agbi, 2009; Zvolensky, McMillan, Gonzalez, & Asmundson, 2010).[9] Mental health issues such as depression have been shown to be more prevalent among chronic low back pain sufferers than the rest of the population (Dahan et al., 2014) and this correlation could be particularly pronounced among the over-50s (Park et al., 2018).

It is clear that the social determinants of health ought to be considered for each case; indeed, the necessity to 'consider the patient as a whole' is outlined in Standard B1 (General Osteopathic Practice Council, 2012, p. 9). Chronic low back pain is a complex complaint, and I feel that in the past I may have focussed more on the specific complexities of the anatomy and not given due attention to associated factors. As a result of my research, I am keen to continue identifying the associated psychosocial factors for sufferers of chronic low back pain as such consideration leads to holistic best practice and ultimately better patient outcomes.

This assignment has presented three patches, written during the course of my second year of university. Each patch has been used as a point for exploration around the themes of assertiveness, communication, and a common patient complaint, chronic low back pain. By exploring each, I have been able to identify specific elements of my personal and professional development on which I can focus, and this will ultimately improve patient outcomes.[10]

References

Alkherayf, F., & Agbi, C. (2009). Cigarette smoking and chronic low back pain in the adult population. *Clinical and Investigative Medicine, 32*(5), E360–E367.

Balague, F, Mannion, F., & Cedraschi, C. (2011). Non-specific low back pain. *The Lancet, 379*, 482–491.

9 Supporting and explorative sentences.

10 The conclusion briefly summarises the content and shows how the question has been addressed.

Balzar-Riley, J. (2012) *Communication in nursing*. St. Louis, MS: Elsevier/Mosby.

Cohen, S., & Hooten, W., (2017). Advances in the diagnosis and management of neck pain. *British Medical Journal, 358*, j3221.

Flying Start NHS (2018). *Assertiveness*. [online] Available at: http://www.flyingstart.scot.nhs.uk/learning-programmes/communication/assertiveness/

Harley, J. (2014). Developing assertiveness skills for health and social care professionals. *Nursing Management, 20*(10), 17.

Hodgetts, J. (2011). Being assertive benefits everyone. *Nursing Times*. [online] Available at: https://www.nursingtimes.net/roles/nurse-managers/being-assertive-benefits-everyone/5038545.article

Hoy, D., March, L., Brooks, P., Blyth, F., Woolf, A., Bain, C., ..., Buchbinder, R. (2014). The global burden of low back pain. *Annals of the Rheumatic Diseases, 73*(6), 968–974.

IpAC. (n.d.). *Assertive communication: Making yourself heard in a health care team*. [online] Available at: https://moodle.une.edu.au/pluginfile.php/452247/mod_data/intro/User-Manual-Assertive-communication-FINAL.pdf

Leach, K. (Ed.). (2011). *Communicating risk of treatment and informed consent in osteopathic practice*. University of Brighton. [online] Available at: http://www.ncor.org.uk/wp-content/uploads/2012/10/communicating-risk.pdf

Lewis, K., Farber, S., Chen, H., & Peska, D. (2015). Learning with reflection: Practices in an osteopathic surgery clinical clerkship through an online module. *The Journal of the American Osteopathic Association, 115*(11), 678–685.

Morley, K. (2016). Nurofen advert banned for misleading claims on joint and back pain. *The Telegraph*. [online] Available at: https://www.telegraph.co.uk/news/2016/06/28/nurofen-advert-banned-for-misleading-claims-on-joint-and-back-pa/

Orrock, P., & Myers, S. (2013). Osteopathic intervention in chronic non-specific low back pain: A systematic review. *BMC Musculoskeletal Disorders, 14*, 129.

Park, S., Kim, H., Jang, S., Kim, H., Chang, B., Lee, C., & Yeom, J. S. (2018). Depression is closely associated with chronic low back pain in patients over 50 years of age: A cross-sectional study using the sixth Korea national health and nutrition examination survey. *Spine, 43*(18), 1281–1288.

Smith, L., & Winter, R. (2003). Applied epistemology for community nurses: Evaluating the impact of the patchwork text. *Innovations in Education and Teaching International, 40*(2), 161–173.

Spadaccini, J., & Esteves, J. (2014). Intuition, analysis and reflection: An experimental study into the decision-making processes and thinking dispositions of osteopathy students. *International Journal of Osteopathic* Medicine, *17*(4), 263–271.

Travaline, J., Ruchinskas, R., & D'Alonzo, G. (2005). Patient-physician communication: Why and how. *The Journal of the American Osteopathic Association, 105*, 13–18.

Winter, R. (2003). "Surface learning": The patchwork text as a remedy for the academic essay. *The Guardian*, Education Section.

Zvolensky, M., McMillan, K., Gonzalez, A., & Asmundson, G. (2010). Chronic musculoskeletal pain and cigarette smoking among a representative sample of Canadian adolescents and adults. *Addictive Behaviors, 35*(11), 1008–1012.

Assignment 3

Critically reflect on an incident from a recent placement

Introduction

This reflective essay will examine a critical incident in which the private data of a patient was compromised. In healthcare, data security means 'data that has been legitimately collected about a person should be protected by all reasonable and appropriate measures against loss, degradation, unauthorised destruction, access, use, manipulation, modification or communication' (Kluge, 2003, p. 8). Healthcare workers have the responsibility to be aware of the policies of their institution and to act in accordance with them (Kline & Khan, 2013; NDG, 2016).[1] However, the incident upon which I reflect in this essay led me to consider how this is not always the case, and that data security policy may be breached for a number of reasons. This led me to the question of how breach of data security policy affects a healthcare worker's duty of care to their patients.

Reflection is an important part of any healthcare professional's learning as it enables practitioners to see their experiences in a new way and to decide consciously on their future courses of action (Jasper, 2013). This essay will use Kolb's reflective cycle (1984) as it provides a clear structure for outlining the events, my learning, and engagement with relevant literature, and my intentions going forwards (Kolb, 1984).[2]

In accordance with NMC guidelines (2018), all individuals referred to within the essay remain anonymous.

Concrete incident

I was working as a secretary within a maternity care unit. Part of my role was to file patient records and pass them on to the patients' GPs once they had been removed from our care. It happened that one of the junior doctor's wives had given birth in the ward and complications meant that

1 Here the student opens with a couple of broad definitions of the main issue to be explored. At this stage they have not mentioned the theme – this will emerge following the description of the incident. Rather, they ground the essay in the subject area from which the theme will emerge. It will depend on your individual choice, the framework you are using and the subject that you are discussing as to whether you choose to follow a similar pattern, or to begin with a definition of the central theme directly. The key is to be aware that both options are possible within an introduction.

2 As is common practice in many reflective assignments, a definition of reflection and its benefits are given.

she had to undergo a series of tests following the birth. On one occasion I was working at front desk when the junior doctor initiated a conversation with my manager. They knew each other outside of work and had a good relationship. He mentioned how they had not been notified regarding the results of their test. He said that this was a source of stress, particularly for his wife. My colleague spontaneously mentioned that we could probably access the results here as his wife would be on file. He said that this would be very much appreciated and would help relieve a lot of stress. As my manager searched for the file, the junior doctor came behind the desk and approached the computer. My manager began clicking through the records to access the patient's details. As she did, I questioned her[3] and said that I thought that the policy was that records were not supposed to be shown to anyone other than the patient without them being present. My manager replied that in this case she thought it would be acceptable. The junior doctor, however, interjected, saying that he did not want to cause any potential problems and would be happy to wait. He left and I immediately apologised to my manager. She told me not to apologise and that in hindsight she saw my response had been correct.

Observation and reflection

Overhearing the conversation between the junior doctor and my manager, I could not help but feel sympathy for the junior doctor and his wife. He was already back at work, with a very young baby at home and the situation with the delayed test results was obviously a cause of distress. Part of my role is to answer the phone and field complaints from other patients when similar situations occur, but this was the first time I had seen first-hand the distress this can cause. I reflected that while it may be simple to respond to patient complaints with annoyance, for each complaint there is an individual probably suffering similar stress to that suffered by the junior doctor.

When I heard my manager offering to show the junior doctor his wife's records, I began to feel uncomfortable. I knew from my training on patient data privacy that this was against the fundamentals of what the

---

3 In many reflective models, you will be asked to provide a description separate from your feelings or opinions at the time. This may seem unnatural, as in most narratives we are used to understanding someone's motivations. Here, for example, it seems odd that the writer does not tell us why she acted. This is a quirk of many reflective models that can take some getting used to. However, having a clear, chronological list of the facts, presented in this objective fashion is useful as it gives you the opportunity to revisit each stage of the event in further sections of the assignment. In many ways, the description of events acts as a 'frame' onto which you can hang the more analytical and evaluative elements of your assignment.

policies are put in place for: to uphold individual liberties (General Data Protection Regulation, 2018). This was a cause of internal conflict for me. I could understand my manager's motivations; she knew the doctor and his wife, and genuinely wanted to help. I also assumed that she would have made her decision based on her knowledge of the junior doctor and his wife. However, at the same time I recalled from my training that even when the situation seems harmless regulations should be upheld, as we know that the reasons behind someone wanting to access another's records may not be obvious.

I knew I should confront my manager about her intention to access the confidential records, but I felt extremely nervous about doing so. Luckily, I did not have too much time to think about it; if I had, I think my nerves may have prevented me. I posed the challenge as a question rather than a statement, in order to avoid appearing too confrontational. When my manager replied that she thought it would be fine in this case I could see that she was a little annoyed to have been challenged and for a moment I regretted my decision to ask. However, when the junior doctor agreed with me and retreated I felt very grateful. Even if my speaking up had caused a little tension between my manager and I, I felt content that my decision was justified. This was confirmed when I apologised to my manager and she agreed that I had done the right thing.

Abstract conceptualisation

Upon reflection, the key theme that emerges from this incident was our duty of care as healthcare professionals to our patients.[4] This manifested in two ways: firstly, by recognising how the policies around data security and patient confidentiality are designed to maintain this duty of care. Secondly, on a personal level, I realise how my actions in challenging poor practice were in line with my responsibilities to provide a duty of care to the patient.

Duty of care is a principle that applies to all healthcare professionals, who must ensure that their actions or omissions do not in any way compromise the health or safety of patients (Royal College of Nursing (RCN), 2018). This applies equally to the field of data security as it does to any other area of healthcare (Information Governance Alliance, 2015; Kline

---

4 Here the key theme emerges. The student clearly defines the theme and the reasons why it has been identified. As noted in Chapter 5, finding the key theme can take some time, and it is not always a case of writing about the subject matter (in this case data privacy). Reflection often reveals a deeper layer and in this case the students has linked the two major components – the potential data breach and her reaction to it – to the underlying theme.

& Khan, 2013; Nursing and Midwifery Council (NMC), 2015). In the situation described, our duty of care was to the patient: the junior doctor's wife. As stated by Caldicott (2013), all patients of any healthcare institution should be able to trust that their personal information is stored securely and that every effort is made to protect the information. Furthermore, they should be able to trust that their information is only shared when it is done so in their best interests and with their informed consent.[5]

The first issue to consider is staff's understanding of their responsibilities regarding data security.[6] There are clear policies in place outlining this: according to the General Data Protection Regulations (2018) patient data must be stored securely and institutions are required to have systems to ensure no unlawful or unauthorised access takes place (Article 5) (ICO, 2018c). Staff must undergo training to ensure they understand how to handle patient information both safely and in a way that complies with legislation (NDG, 2016) and are expected to have a thorough understanding of the policies relevant to their particular workplace (Kline & Khan, 2013; NDG, 2016).

However, this is not always the case[7] and policies alone do not always prevent errors or breaches of policy. As noted by Ondiege and Clark (2017), staff are not always fully aware of their responsibilities. This point is reiterated in a report by the Quality Care Commission (2016), which noted that the actions of staff on the ground do not always reflect the data security policies. Lack of knowledge is not the only factor; human behaviour has been shown as one of the most prominent reasons for data security breaches (along with accidental sharing and technological errors) (Edwards, Hofmeyr, & Forrest, 2016; Fernandez-Aleman et al., 2015; NDG, 2016). This behaviour[8] often stems from the fact that data security policies – and healthcare policies in general – are often seen to prevent

5 This paragraph, coming as it does at the beginning of the analytical discussion, outlines the fundamental principles of the key theme. See Chapters 12–14 – Linking Theory to Practice – for tips on this.

6 Notice how the student is using clear topic sentences to guide the reader through the assignment and signpost what is coming next. The simple phrase 'the first issue to consider...' does a lot of work, firstly signalling we are now moving away from definitions of duty of care and secondly, signalling that we can expect analysis from a second angle later on.

7 The writer moves from descriptive to analytical here. Now we are looking at criticism of the ideas noted, comparing them to real world studies.

8 Note the use of cohesive devices throughout this paragraph as the writer synthesises the ideas. We have demonstrative pronouns: 'This point...'; synonyms: 'not always aware of/lack of knowledge'; repetition of keywords: 'behaviour' and transition words; 'Therefore'. All these are doing important work, guiding the reader through the ideas.

healthcare professionals from giving the best care that they can to their patients. Therefore, many will look for 'workarounds' (NDG, 2016; Stahl, Doherty, & Shaw, 2011).

This was certainly the case in the scenario described; my manager's intentions were to alleviate the stress of her colleague.[9] The problem, however, is that by doing this a patient's private data was at risk of being seen by someone who was not legally authorised to do so. Anyone in charge of sensitive data is legally obliged to see only the material it is necessary for them to see, and to ensure that the integrity of the information is not compromised (Department of Health, 2003; ICO, 2018b; Stahl, Doherty, & Shaw, 2011). My manager would have been breaking both guidelines if she had continued to access the file of the junior doctor's wife. Breaking these guidelines would, in effect, have constituted a breach of duty of care to a hospital patient.

While I have been aware of policy since my training, this incident caused me to understand the link between these policies and our duty of care to our patients. The situation has clarified to me that regulations are put in place with good reason, and relate back to the central tenant of healthcare: our duty of care to our patients (NMC, 2016) While I have never knowingly broken rules, this reflection has confirmed to me the importance of keeping up to date with policy, and attending refresher training at regular intervals.[10]

Just as my manager would have been breaking her duty of care to her patient if she had continued to access the file, I would have been complicit had I not challenged the poor practice. As noted earlier, in order to uphold our duty of care we must ensure that our "actions *or omissions*" [my italics] do not compromise the safety of our patients (Royal College of Nursing (RCN), 2018).

One key role of any healthcare practitioner who works with health informatics is to help others achieve the strict standards governing patient information (Kluge, 2003). Standard 3.4 of the NMC code clearly outlines the healthcare professional's responsibility to question poor practice (NMC, 2015). This means raising any concerns and acting to correct the problem as quickly as possible (NMC, 2015). As noted by Kline and Khan (2013), whenever poor practice is suspected, the healthcare worker's duty

9 The writer ties the theory back to the critical incident. It can be easy to forget this once you have switched to a more analytical style, but it is key to show that you are constantly reflecting on what the literature means for your reflection.

10 The writer provides a summary of the key learnings from the first issue, before moving on to the second.

is to the patient, and every practitioner must learn to see speaking up for their patients as an essential part of their role (NMC, 2017b).

Of course, this is not always easy in practice. In my case I was challenging a superior, with whom I worked closely and often alone on a daily basis. Any challenge to a fellow professional may not be taken well (North West Dignity Leads Network, 2014; NMC, 2017), and this felt particularly true in this case. For this reason, I posed my challenge as a question, which instinctively felt like the right thing to do. Having looked into the matter further[11], it seems my approach was correct; as outlined by Kline and Khan (2013) the goal when questioning poor practice should be to understand and support the colleague being challenged. Remaining polite and respecting the colleague are important features of a successful challenge (North West Dignity Leads Network, 2014). My colleague's acceptance and lack of defensiveness justified my approach. Recognising that the patient's duty of care was at risk and speaking up enabled a positive outcome from a potentially negative situation. It confirmed my feeling that even though I was a junior member of staff, I have a duty to speak out should I encounter poor practice.

My experience challenging poor practice has led me to realise that there may be other situations in which I may have to speak up. In this case, my manager's admission that in hindsight I was probably correct demonstrated that her error could have stemmed from a lack of adequate knowledge around the subject. As noted previously, this is common and defined by Kline and Khan (2013) as an 'inadvertent' error. They list other types of behaviours that should be challenged as 'at risk' behaviour, in which the practitioner does not realise they are putting the patient at risk, and 'reckless' behaviour, in which the practitioner knows that an action is not correct but proceeds regardless. As I grow and progress in my career, I will make an effort to recognise these behaviours and develop appropriate techniques for dealing with each.

Active experimentation

This incident on which I have reflected had the potential to be a negative one. Firstly, because a breach of a patient's data could easily have occurred, and secondly, because in speaking up I may have harmed my relationship with my manager. Luckily, neither of these situations came to pass and our duty of care to the patient was upheld.

---

11 Here the writer demonstrates the result of her reflection, namely, that the incident has forced her to look into the matter more closely. We get a sense of how he has responded to the incident and that the purpose of reflection has been achieved; to further her understanding of her role.

This reflection has led me to see the real value in the policies that govern any healthcare institution, and recognise why they should be adhered to. My commitment henceforth is to maintain a sound knowledge of policy guidelines, not just around data security, but all other aspects of my profession. I have also learned that despite my apprehension about doing so, speaking out was the right thing to do. I honoured my responsibility to my patient, but also to my colleague as I prevented her from committing a potential breach of privacy. I realise now that I need not be nervous or unsure if I am challenging poor practice that goes against policy I know to be true. This reflection has encouraged me to examine further the reasons why people may breach policy, but also to consider techniques for challenging it. Therefore one concrete goal that has come from this reflection is a commitment to attend CPD courses in areas for personal development such as assertiveness training and emotional intelligence.[12]

Overall, I feel proud that I acted in the correct way and I will use this as an important confidence builder as I move forward in my career.

References

Caldicott, F. (2013). *Information: To share or not to share? the information governance review*. London, UK: Department of Health. Retrieved November 5, 2018, from https://assets.publishing.service.gov.uk/government/uploads/system/uploads/attachment_data/file/192572/2900774_InfoGovernance_accv2.pdf

Care Quality Commission. (2016). *Safe data, safe care: Report into how data is safely and securely managed in the NHS*. Retrieved November 5, 2018, from https://www.cqc.org.uk/sites/default/files/20160701%20Data%20security%20review%20FINAL%20for%20web.pdf

Department of Health. (2003). *Confidentiality NHS Code of Practice.* Retrieved November 11, 2018, from https://assets.publishing.service.gov.uk/government/uploads/system/uploads/attachment_data/file/200146/Confidentiality_-_NHS_Code_of_Practice.pdf

Edwards, B., Hofmeyr, S., & Forrest, S. (2016). Hype and heavy tails: A closer look at data breaches, *Journal of Cybersecurity, 2*(1), 3–14. Retrieved November 21, 2018, from https://academic.oup.com/cybersecurity/article/2/1/3/2736315

European Commission. (2018). *General Data Protection Regulation (GDPR).* Retrieved November 24, 2018, from https://ec.europa.eu/commission/priorities/justice-and-fundamental-rights/data-protection/2018-reform-eu-data-protection-rules_en

Fernandez-Aleman, J. L., Sanchez-Henarejos, A., Toval, A., Sánchez-García, A. B., Hernández-Hernández, I., & Fernandez-Luque, L. (2015). Analysis of health

12 The writer outlines a clear plan of action following her reflection.

professional security behaviors in a real clinical setting: An empirical study. *International Journal of Medical Informatics, 84*(6), 454–467. Retrieved November 21, 2018, from https://www.sciencedirect.com/science/article/pii/S1386505615000131?via%3Dihub

Information Commissioner's Office. (ICO). (2014). Cited in National Data Guardian for Health and Care (NDG). (2016). *Review of data security, consent and opt-outs.* Retrieved November 9, 2018, from https://assets.publishing.service.gov.uk/government/uploads/system/uploads/attachment_data/file/535024/data-security-review.PDF

Information Commissioner's Office. (2018a). *Data security incident trends.* Retrieved November 21, 2018, from https://ico.org.uk/action-weve-taken/data-security-incident-trends/

Information Commissioner's Office (ICO). (2018b). *Security.* Retrieved November 5, 2018, from https://ico.org.uk/for-organisations/guide-to-the-general-data-protection-regulation-gdpr/security/

Information Commissioner's Office. (ICO). (2018c). *Guide to the General Data Protection Regulation (GDPR).* Retrieved November 5, 2018, from https://ico.org.uk/for-organisations/guide-to-the-general-data-protection-regulation-gdpr

Information Governance Alliance. (2015). *The duty of care.* Retrieved November 5, 2018, from https://www.igt.hscic.gov.uk/Resources/The%20Duty%20of%20Care.pdf

Ismail, M. (2014). *User compliance to information security policy* (Order No. 1554439). (1527125667). Retrieved November 11, 2018, from https://search.proquest.com/docview/1527125667?accountid=14680

Jasper, M. (2013). *Beginning reflective practice* (2nd ed.). Andover, MA: Cengage.

Kline, R., & Khan, S. (2013). *The duty of care of health professionals: A handbook.* London, UK: Public World. Retrieved November 11, 2018, from http://www.publicworld.org/files/Duty_of_Care_handbook_April_2013.pdf

Kluge, E.-H. (2003). *A handbook of ethics for health informatics professionals.* The British Computer Society Health Informatics Committee. Bristol, UK: Arrowsmith Ltd.

National Data Guardian for Health and Care. (NDG). (2016). *Review of data security, consent and opt-outs.* Retrieved November 9, 2018, from https://assets.publishing.service.gov.uk/government/uploads/system/uploads/attachment_data/file/535024/data-security-review.PDF

North West Dignity Leads Network. (2014). *Challenging poor practice: Training module.* Retrieved November 24, 2018, from https://www.dignityincare.org.uk/_assets/Challenging_Booklet_low_res.pdf

Nursing and Midwifery Council. (2015). *The Code: Professional standards of practice and behaviour for nurses, midwives and nursing associates.* London, UK: Nursing & Midwifery Council. Retrieved November 11, 2018, from https://www.nmc.org.uk/globalassets/sitedocuments/nmc-publications/nmc-code.pdf

Nursing and Midwifery Council. (2017a). *Enabling professionalism in nursing and midwifery practice.* London, UK: Nursing & Midwifery Council. Retrieved

November 24, 2018, from https://www.nmc.org.uk/globalassets/sitedocuments/other-publications/enabling-professionalism.pdf

Nursing and Midwifery Council. (2017b). *Raising concerns guidance for nurses and midwives*. London, UK: Nursing & Midwifery Council. Retrieved November 11, 2018, from https://www.nmc.org.uk/globalassets/blocks/media-block/raising-concerns-v2.pdf

Ondiege, B., & Clarke, M. (2017). Health care professionals' perception of security of personal health devices. *Smart Homecare Technology and Telehealth, 2017*(4), 35–42.

Petersen, C., Berner, E. S., Embi, P. J., Hollis, K. F., Goodman, K. W., Koppel, R., ..., Winkelstein, P. (2018). AMIA's code of professional and ethical conduct 2018. *Journal of the American Medical Informatics Association, 25*(11), 1579–1582.

Royal College of Nursing. (2018). *Duty of care: Advice guides*. Retrieved November 5, 2018, from file:///Users/helenhumphreys/Downloads/Duty%20of%20care.pdf

Stahl, B. C., Doherty N. F., & Shaw, M. (2011). Information security policies in the UK healthcare sector: A critical evaluation. *Information Systems Journal, 22*(1), 77–94.

APPENDIX

2

Quick Grammar Guide

Your lecturers may provide the technical terms for some punctuation errors they see in your work. Because of this, the following errors have been given their technical terms together with an explanation on the nature of the error and how to avoid it.

The comma splice

One of the most common grammatical mistakes is the ***comma splice***. A comma splice occurs when a writer joins two ***independent clauses*** together with a comma. Consider the below for an example of a comma splice:

I walked into the clinic, I felt exhausted.

Think about the word ***independent*** here – what does it mean to you? Does something which is independent need anything else, or can it stand alone?

There are two clauses in this statement and both are independent. An independent clause is one which can be a sentence in its own right. For example, say to yourself: 'I walked into the clinic'. You could put a full stop at the end of that statement and that would be that. You walked into the clinic.

Likewise, 'I felt exhausted' is also a sentence in its own right. Say it to yourself: 'I felt exhausted'. You could have a full stop at the end of that too.

Contrast these independent clauses with a *dependent* clause:

While I was working at placement

Now, if you say this sentence to yourself you are left with a question – something along the lines of 'what happened while you were working at placement?' Would you happily put a full stop at the end of this statement? No. The fact that you need more information should indicate that what you are looking at is a ***dependent*** clause – it needs something else for it to make sense. As it happens, it needs an independent clause (e.g. I was mentored by Dave).

Your task when deciding how to punctuate should be based on the clause types present. If you can say both clauses as sentences in their own right, then you should be using a linker such as 'and' or a full stop or in some cases a semicolon or a colon. **But if you join two independent clauses with a comma, that's a comma splice**.

The sentence fragment

Fragmented sentences are another common problem in written submissions. They can happen for a number of reasons and this section will explain what they are, how to spot them and how to avoid them.

A sentence fragment is an **incomplete sentence.** Most often, sentences like this are in a 'note form' and have been written by students rushing to meet deadlines. Consider the following example:

> I went to check Mr Jones – blood pressure 120/80 mmhg.

Or

> Then took oxygen saturation reading. Pulse was bradycardic 57 bpm.

Here, the student has transferred their case notes into an essay, and while there may be times that you can do this you should try to present academic writing in full sentences so that you most clearly express your points to the marker.

When making notes while you read (or are on a placement as in the example) it is good practice that these are **notes** (and not necessarily full sentences). When writing an assignment, however, you should *expand on these notes* so that your ideas are expressed clearly and through sentences which leave little room for the reader to misunderstand.

To update the previous examples:

> I went to check Mr Jones' blood pressure, which read 120/80 mmhg. Following this, I took an oxygen saturation reading.

The dangling modifier

Dangling modifiers are **misplaced or missing pieces of information** which obscure the meaning of what you are trying to communicate.

> Noticing Mr Jones' anxiety, his temperature was taken again.

This is a dangling modifier. Read it again carefully. We can suppose that the writer is trying to communicate that they took Mr Jones' temperature in an attempt to relieve his anxiety – but what they've written does not mean that. What is written actually means that Mr Jones' temperature noticed his anxiety (which, we're sure you'll agree is really confusing).

To overcome such issues, the writer should reword the sentence by adding information, or moving it closer to the thing it is related to:

> Noticing Mr Jones' anxiety, I took his temperature again.

To avoid making these kinds of mistakes with your writing, you need to carefully read your work and think about what you've written actually means. This can take practice, but try to put yourself in your reader's position – all they have are the words on the page.

The run-on sentence

Run-on sentences are those which combine **grammatical clauses** and do not use **conjunctions** (i.e. and/or/but/however) effectively. First, let's consider a **grammatical clause:**

This is part of a sentence which expresses an idea – e.g.:

> The semi-circular canals are located in the inner ear

If the writer was to combine this clause with another, e.g.:

> They provide sensory information about rotary movements

he or she should use a **conjunction** (or a punctuation mark) to join (or separate) these clauses. However, in some cases, the writer may not do this which leads to a run-on sentence. For example:

> The semi-circular canals are located in the inner ear they provide sensory information about rotary movements

In the above example, the use of an effective conjunction (or punctuation) would help the writer to make their point more clearly (and grammatically accurately). For example:

> The semi-circular canals are located in the inner ear. They provide sensory information about rotary movements

In the above example, the student may actually be better off combining the ideas into a neater, more efficient sentence:

> The semi-circular canals, which provide sensory information about rotary movements, are located in the inner ear.

APPENDIX

3

Feedback Glossary

Here you will find some of the most common feedback comments that your lecturer might make on your work, along with explanations of what they might mean. Where applicable, directions are provided to the relevant chapter of this book in which you may be able to find ways to resolve the issue.

Structure is unclear

This is one of the most common issues we see within student work. While students may have a good understanding of all the ideas, if these are not structured well then the effect is a paper that is very difficult to read. One simple remedy to this is to see your role as a guide: you need to 'walk' your reader through your ideas, enabling them clearly to see what is coming next. This is true for the whole assignment – your paragraphs need to be structured in a logical order with clear topic sentences – but also within each paragraph, where you need to ensure your writing flows.

See: Chapters 6, 7, 9, 10, 11 and 14

Run-on sentence

A common feature of many students' writing is that in order to sound 'academic' they attempt to cram a lot of information into a sentence. Too often, this is at the expense of clarity. Remember, the most important feature of good academic writing is that it is easy to understand the ideas presented. Break up sentences to ensure each point you are making is clear.

See: Quick Grammar Guide in Appendix 2

This information is not appropriate in this section

The reflective writing frameworks can feel a little prescriptive and even unnatural at times. For example, the separation of action from your thoughts and feelings is not something that would usually occur when relating an event. Make sure you have a clear understanding of what is required of each section before you begin. Knowing whether you are expected to use first or third person, whether you are expected to include references, and even how long each particular section is supposed to be can help avoid this error.

See: Chapter 6

Writing is too descriptive

You may receive this feedback if your lecturer feels that you have not engaged critically enough with the literature. If your assignment calls for critical analysis, you are required to do more than simply list the facts and definitions. You should consider how different theories and ideas relate to each other, and what this might mean, both for you personally but also on the scale of more general practice.

See: Chapter 14

Style not appropriate

Even though reflective writing can seem akin to diary writing at times, you are expected to maintain an academic 'register' throughout your work. There are certain conventions which govern what is considered appropriately academic. These may seem intimidating, but in fact learning a few simple rules and principles will ensure you write in the manner required for academia.

See: Chapter 8

Unnecessary word/phrase

Students often fall into the trap of using five words where one will do. This is very natural – in speaking we do it all the time to ensure our listener understands us. In writing we can afford to be more concise. Eliminating redundancy often comes at the editing stage (handy if you need to reduce your word count!). Ask yourself: Is there a neater way I can say this? If I took this away would it change the meaning? Your first draft will almost always require some cutting. Build the process into your writing habit.

See: Chapter 8

Meaning is not clear

This can be for a number of reasons: incorrect grammar, a wrong choice of words or a lack of structure. It may occur because the writer does not fully understand the information they are trying to convey, or because they are attempting to make it sound too wordy and 'academic'. To avoid this, think really carefully about each point you want to make. Remember: clarity is key, so make the point in a simple way if it helps.

Not your own words

This feedback is every student's nightmare. If plagiarism is spotted it can mean a lowered grade, a resubmission or at worst, expulsion from the institution. The large majority of plagiarism is unintentional and stems from students not knowing the extent to which they have to change the original texts they read. Getting a good grasp of quoting, paraphrasing and referencing techniques will help avoid this.

See: Chapter 13

Answers

Exercise 6.1 Suggested answer

Notes from the Social Work assignment divided into the six steps from Gibbs' Reflective Cycle.

Description

Role-play – foster care child assessment
Entered the room
Appearance of child – burn marks
Questions – no response
Arlene – picture prompts and three wishes – better response
Scared of dog – wants to stay with family

What happened?
Who was there?
What was my role in what happened?

Thoughts and feelings

Before and during: nervous
During: shocked/embarrassed
Afterwards: ashamed

Evaluation

Positive: Arlene's explanation of process/eye contact/picture prompts and success in finding out about Jenny's feelings
Negative: my own lack of ability to get information needed. No explanation/lack of eye contact/had only prepared structured interview

What was positive/negative about the situation?
Why did the events happen?

Analysis

Key theme: Child-centred communication.
Subthemes:

- transparency/trust
- body language
- methods of communication for developmental stages

Why did I behave as I did?
Why did others behave in the way that they did?

Conclusion

Learned about importance of child-centred communication
Could have improved own techniques (transparency/non-verbal communication/different methods of communication)

Do differently next time: explanation/body language/ prepare developmentally appropriate methods of communication/resources/play
I can be uncomfortable/nervous in a new situation – need to put these feelings aside to focus on service user

What does the literature have to say about why the events happened?

Action plan

In future: introductions/explanation of plan/concentrate on own body language/prepare resources for communication

Exercise 6.2 Suggested answer

Concrete experience

Role-play – foster care child assessment
Appearance of child – burn marks
My structures questions – no response
Arlene – picture prompts and three wishes – better response
Scared of dog – wants to stay with family

Observation and reflection

Before and during: nervous
During: shocked/embarrassed
Afterwards: ashamed
Positive: Arlene's explanation of process/eye contact/picture prompts and success in finding out about Jenny's feelings.
Negative: my own lack of ability to get information needed.
No explanation/lack of eye contact/had only prepared structured interview

What can I learn from why I behaved as I did/why others behaved in the way that they did?

Abstract conceptualisation

Key theme: Child-centred communication.
Subthemes:

- Transparency/trust
- Body language
- Methods of communication for developmental stages

How can I change my practice based on my reflections on this experience?

Active experimentation

In future: introductions/explanation of plan/concentrate on own body language/prepare resources for communication
Reading up on communication with vulnerable children (refs)

How have I changed my practice already based on my learning from these reflections?

Exercise 8.1

The head nurse was behind schedule for Mr. Barnard's morning injection. I had arrived before her so I entered his cubicle and talked with him for a short time until the nurse arrived. I asked how his day had been and which TV programmes he liked to watch. As we talked I observed a change in his demeanour. His speech became slower then he began to stutter. His head dropped to his chest and he stopped talking altogether. I looked out of the cubicle but the head nurse was nowhere to be seen so I called out for help. I remembered that there was a panic button next to Mr. Barnard's bed. ~~That was really stupid of me to forget that.~~ I ran to the button and pressed it. ~~It was all a bit of a blur, but~~ I picked up Mr. Barnard's head from his chest and checked his Airway, Breathing and Circulation (ABC) He was still breathing and there was no blockage. Two senior nurses came into the room and I told them everything ~~what~~ I knew and they took over. I stepped back and watched, and as I did, Mr. Barnard regained consciousness. The nurses asked him questions such as could he remember the day ~~and things like that~~, which he answered correctly.

Explanations

Behind schedule – 'running late' is too colloquial (the literal meaning of 'running' is not the same as the intended meaning here). Also avoid using phrases such as 'a bit' as they do not add anything to the overall meaning.

I had arrived before her, – this is much more appropriate than 'at a loose end' and relays the situation equally as accurately.

Talked – One thing any academic writing aims for is to be as concise and precise as possible. 'Talked' achieved in one word what 'had a chat' does in three, and it is much more precise as well.

A short time – One key feature of academic writing is accuracy, and it is almost always advisable to give a precise figure where possible. In this situation, however, 'a short while' is more appropriate, as it is unlikely that the student would have recorded the exact time they were talking, and unnecessary to give this information.

I asked – 'made small talk' is very colloquial language again – the literal meaning is not clear. The student would be clearer if they replaced the whole first clause (part of the sentence) with simply: 'I asked…'

A change in his demeanour – 'Came over all funny' may well be how the student would describe this to a friend, but if we examine the words more closely it's not clear what happened. The purpose of this sentence is to prepare us for how his behaviour changed – 'change in his demeanour' achieves the same function in a more academic tone.

He began to stutter – 'Started to stutter' would be fine as well; the key thing here is the removal of 'just'. This would be very common in speech, but it serves little or no purpose in helping us understand the content of this sentence.

Looked – This is less wordy than 'stuck my head out' and more accurately describes the important action.

I remembered – More accurate than the literal meaning of 'it struck me' (and less painful!)

Airway, breathing and circulation – Even if you are certain that the reader of your assignment will understand technical acronyms, it is always better to write these in full the first time you use them. You should then place the acronym in parentheses directly afterwards, and use the acronym from here.

Regained consciousness – Phrasal verbs (or 'two part verbs') such as 'came round', 'put off', 'look into' will always have a more accurate single verb.

Such as – this is better than 'like' for giving examples.

Note:

'then he just started to stutter, just going over the same sounds over and over again'

You may have noticed the redundancy here – there was no need for the writer to explain the meaning of 'stutter' so ' **'just going over the same sounds over and over again'** has been deleted from the original text as well.

Repetition of words:

X states...

The writer uses the same reporting verb to introduce the literature. They could improve the work by varying these throughout the paragraph. See Chapter 13 for some ideas on reporting verbs.

Repetition of ideas:

Marsden (2006) states that this may cause them to put up an instant barrier. Jones (2004) suggests that negative body language can cause patients to feel reluctant to communicate with a paramedic.

The ideas expressed in these two sentences are very similar – the writer should consider combining them or choosing the most appropriate source.

Informality:

Obviously...

Colloquial, unnecessary language that could be deleted.

Give off, put up, break down

Use of phrasal verbs – 'convey', 'construct', and 'eliminate' might be more appropriate academic terms here.

Redundancy:

all members of the paramedic team

If we remove 'all members' the meaning of the sentence does not change. When we read 'paramedic team' we infer that the writer means all members of the team.

...which does not convey negative feelings.

The writer is over-explaining the point here. Neutral body language, by its very nature, does not convey any negative feelings.

Exercise 9.1

i. *Demonstrate the relevance of your topic.*
ii. *Contextualise your assignment.*
iii. *Eliminate surprise by guiding your reader through the rest of your assignment.*
iv. *Include any other statements which your assignment guidelines require.* Check your assignment guidelines for further instruction.

Dignity is a key concept in nursing and integral to the Nursing and Midwifery Code of Practice. The NMC states that in prioritising people, its members should 'Treat people as individuals and uphold their dignity' (NMC, 2018). *(i)*

Dignity is a complex concept which can be viewed from different perspectives. The Royal College of Nursing defines dignity as '*concerned with how people feel, think and behave in relation to the worth or value of themselves and others. To treat someone with dignity is to treat them as being of worth, in a way that is respectful of them as valued individuals*' (RCN, 2008), thus alluding to both the physical and relational aspects of dignity. Research has suggested that while elderly patients and their relatives place more importance on the physical aspects of care in upholding dignity, healthcare professionals often place more value on the relational aspects (Cairns et al., 2013). There are many competing demands on a nurse's time, and the nurse needs to ensure that both physical and relational dignity remain at the forefront of care, even when under time and other pressures. *(ii)*

This essay discusses the importance of holistic care in upholding dignity and recognises that the physical and the relational elements of dignity cannot be separated. It does this by means of reflecting on an event from my placement on a geriatric ward caring for a 92-year old diabetic amputee. I consider how my understanding of the concept of dignity has been deepened through this reflection. Specifically, I consider dignity as under the NMC code of conduct. The following three elements of upholding dignity are explored: treating patients with compassion; recognising diversity and individual choice and delivering the fundamentals of care. Through this lens I pinpoint emotional intelligence, confidence and decision-making abilities as key areas for my own personal development in order to provide holistic care that upholds dignity.

I use the *What? So what? Now what?* reflection framework put forward by Driscoll (ref), as this allows a clear means of structuring my essay with a number of trigger questions to guide the reflection process. *(iii)*

In accordance with the NMC (2015), all names have been replaced with pseudonyms. *(iv)*

Exercise 10.1

The topic sentence (TS)
Any supporting and explorative sentences (SS)
The concluding sentence (CS)
The transition sentence (TR)

Communication is vital to effective osteopathic practice (TS). Indeed, most complaints made against osteopaths result from poor communication (General Osteopathic Council, 2012). The Osteopathic Practice Standards set out 'communication and patient partnership' as the first of their four themes, and Standard A1 requires the practitioner to 'adapt communication strategies to suit the specific needs of the patient' (General Osteopathic Council, 2012, p. 4). The specific needs of the patient will obviously change relating to different individuals but it is clear that the competent practitioner will have a range of communicative tools which can be used when interacting with patients. In order for selection of the most effective communication strategy, it is first necessary to identify any potential barriers to patient-practitioner communication. Travaline, Ruchinskas and D'Alonzo provide a checklist for the practitioner to consider potential barriers to communication, these are: 'speech ability or language articulation; foreign language spoken; dysphonia; time constraints on physician or patient; unavailability of physician or patient to meet face-to-face; illness; altered mental state; medication effects; cerebral-vascular event; psychologic or emotional distress; gender differences; racial or cultural differences; [or] other' (2005, p. 14). Should any of these barriers be present, then it is the practitioner's duty to employ strategies aimed at overcoming them and while there is no exhaustive collection of strategies, some are outlined by Leach (2011). These strategies include considering how information can be simplified and tailored in terms of size and pace to meet a particular patient's need. As well as this, the practitioner may consider checking the patient's understanding of information by asking questions, and could draw diagrams to aid with this understanding if appropriate (Leach, 2011) (SS). This assignment now moves to the specific points of non-verbal communicative strategies (TR).

Exercise 11.1

i. *Indicate how you have answered the question.*
ii. *Summarise the main points of the assignment.*
iii. *Suggest implications for future theory or practice.*

In sum, through reflecting on an instance from my own practice on the ward, this essay has shown the importance of upholding both the physical and relational aspects of dignity and highlighted the fact that the two cannot be separated. *(ii)* Through deepening my own understanding of the concepts of compassion, individual choice and fundamentals of care in upholding dignity, I have gained a clearer understanding of the importance of holistic care in upholding dignity. *(i)* That is, care that is holistic in terms of relational and physical aspects, and also in terms of the entire multidisciplinary team collaborating. Having undertaken this reflection, I intend to work on three elements of my own practice: my emotional intelligence, my confidence in decision-making, and multidisciplinary working in terms of upholding dignity. *(iii)*

Exercise 12.1 Possible answer

4. When the patient displayed anxiety and was clearly not responding, the nurse did not attempt to alter her communication style, or think to offer an advocate.
3. Poor communication is one of the most common reasons problems occur when a healthcare worker is examining a patient with learning difficulties (MENCAP, 2016).
5. One way to combat communication difficulties is to utilise a range of communication methods, such as visual or written.
2. Doing this demonstrates compassion for the patient, which is one of the 6 Cs introduced by the NMC in 2012. (The others are: care, competence, communication, courage, and commitment.)
6. It also allows a healthcare professional to abide by the NMC Professional Standards Code (2015), which states that all nurses and midwives must 'prioritise people, preserve safety and promote professionalism'.
1. In light of these guidelines, it is clear that fundamental principles of care were not adhered to in this incident.

Exercise 13.1

Doctors must work on the presumption that every adult patient has the capacity to make decisions about the disclosure of his or her personal information (Harris, 2018).

Possible paraphrases:

Doctors should presume that any patient over the age of 18 is capable of deciding whether they would like their personal data to be shared.

Harris (2018) notes that all adult patients should be presumed capable of deciding whether or not to disclose their personal data.

If someone is going to have a major medical procedure, such as an operation, their consent should ideally be secured well in advance, so they have plenty of time to obtain information about the procedure and ask questions (NHS, 2018).

Possible paraphrases:

Patients should be given adequate time to find information and raise concerns with doctors before a major medical procedure. Therefore, it is essential to obtain consent well in advance (NHS, 2018)

Adequate time should be allowed between asking a patient's consent for, and scheduling any major procedure, so that the patient may find out more about the procedure and ask questions of relevant medical staff (NHS, 2018)

Exercise 13.2

Situation for reflection	Theme identified
Patient's notes left on ward	Privacy
• Statistics on how common this may be • Guidelines for correct procedures around patient notes	• Definitions & discussions of privacy
Student nurse left unattended with an aggressive patient	Assertiveness
• Definition of aggression • Statistics on how common incidences of aggression are in hospitals • Guidelines for dealing with aggression • Guidelines as to how a student nurse should be managed	• Definitions & discussions of assertiveness in healthcare context
Umbilical cord issues during birth leading to emergency C-section	Preparedness
• Definition of emergency C-section • Statistics regarding how common this scenario is	• Definitions & discussions of preparedness
Palliative care for lung cancer patient	Emotional Intelligence
• Definition of palliative care • Definition of lung cancer • Statistics around lung cancer – how common is it?	• Definitions & discussions of emotional intelligence

Exercise 14.1

The paragraph moves from broad to specific information: the definition of a general term, a broad claim made by academics, and, finally, a single case study that backs up this claim.

Exercise 14.2

Level 4 **Here, the student relates their practice effectively to the theme of knowledge sharing. They recognise the benefits of it, and provide three relevant sources to back up their point. They end by linking this back to their own practice.**

Level 5 **Here the student is providing a more critical analysis of the main ideas. The student starts to recognise the limitations of the study by Smith, but is able to dismiss these arguments by providing further evidence that supports their own argument. Note also how the focus has shifted from the authors to the studies, as the student begins to engage more with the ideas.**

Level 6 **Now the critical analysis becomes much deeper. The student provides more commentary on the ideas presented, recognising their limitations but still using them to form a coherent conclusion. The synthesis of the ideas is also more fluid – note how Jones' counterargument to Smith's study is incorporated into a sentence that dismisses it.**

Level 7 **Here, the level of analysis of the central ideas is largely the same as the previous level, though the purpose of the analysis has changed. Rather than simply using the evidence to draw a broad conclusion, the student uses it as a basis to develop their own, new approach to the problem. We would assume the work then goes on to provide further evidence for, and examples of the approach they are proposing.**

Further reading

Reflective practice

Howatson-Jones, L. (2016). *Reflective practice in nursing* (3rd ed.). Los Angeles, CA: Sage.

Jasper, M. (2013). *Beginning reflective practice* (2nd ed.). Andover, MI: Cengage Learning.

Models, frameworks and cycles

Driscoll, J. (2007). *Practising clinical supervision: A reflective approach for healthcare professionals* (2nd ed.). Edinburgh, UK: Baillière Tindall Elsevier.

Gibbs, G. (1988). *Learning by doing: A guide to teaching and learning methods.* Oxford, UK: Further Education Unit: Oxford Polytechnic.

Johns, C. (2006). *Engaging reflection in practice: A narrative approach.* Oxford, UK: Blackwell.

Johns, C. (2017). *Becoming a reflective practitioner* (5th ed.). Oxford, UK: Wiley.

Kolb, D. A. (1984). *Experiential learning: Experience as the source of learning and development.* Englewood Cliffs, NJ; London, UK: Prentice-Hall.

Rolfe, G., Freshwater, D., & Jasper, M. (2001). *Critical reflection for nursing and the helping professions: A user's guide.* London: Red Globe Press.

Schön, D. A. (1983). *The reflective practitioner: How professionals think in action.* New York, NY: Basic Books.

Books on writing/reflective writing

Bassot, B. (2016). *The reflective journal* (2nd ed.). London, UK: Red Globe Press.

Bolton, G. (2010). *Reflective practice: Writing and professional development* (3rd ed.). London, UK: Sage.

Gimenez, J. (2018). *Writing for nursing and midwifery students* (3rd ed.). London, UK: Red Globe Press.

Williams, K., Woolliams, M., & Spiro, J. (2012). *Reflective writing.* London, UK: Red Globe Press.

Study skills

Cottrell, S. (2019). *The study skills handbook* (5th ed.). London, UK: Red Globe Press.

Bibliography

Bassot, B. (2016). *The reflective journal* (2nd ed.). London: Red Globe Press.

Bredesen, D. (2017). *The end of Alzheimer's*. New York, NY: Avery.

Bloom, B. S. (1956). *Taxonomy of education objectives book 1 – Cognitive domain*. New York, NY: David McKay Co.

Borton, T. (1970). *Reach, touch, and teach: Student concerns and process education*. New York, NY: McGraw-Hill.

College of Paramedics. (2017). *Paramedic – Scope of practice policy*. Bridgwater, UK: College of Paramedics.

Davies, M. (1985). *Essential social worker: A guide to positive practice* (2nd ed.). London, UK: Ashgate.

Dewey, J. (1933). *How we think: A restatement of the relation of reflective thinking to the educative process*. Chicago, IL: Henry Regnery Co.

Driscoll, J. (2007). *Practising clinical supervision: A reflective approach for healthcare professionals* (2nd ed.). Edinburgh, UK: Baillière Tindall Elsevier.

Gaisford, M. (2017). Informed consent in paramedic practice. *Journal of Paramedic Practice*, 9, 80–85.

Gibbs, G. (1988). *Learning by doing: A guide to teaching and learning methods*. Oxford, UK: Further Education Unit, Oxford Polytechnic.

Help the Aged. (2001). Towards dignity: Acting on the lessons from hospital experiences of black and minority ethnic older people. In Institute on Aging and Ethnicity (Ed.), *Policy research*. London, UK: Help the Aged.

Jasper, M. (2013). *Beginning reflective practice* (2nd ed.). Andover, MI: Cengage Learning.

Johns, C. (2017). *Becoming a reflective practitioner* (5th ed.). Oxford, UK: Wiley.

Jones, K. (2008). *Best practice in social work: Critical perspectives*. Basingstoke, UK: Palgrave.

Kackperk, L. (2014). Non-verbal communication: The importance of listening. *British Journal of Medicine*, 65, 275–279.

Kernisan, L. (2018). *4 medications to treat Alzheimers & other demantias: How they work and FAQs*. Retrieved from https://betterhealthwhileaging.net/faqs-medications-for-alzheimers-dementia/.

Kolb, D. A. (1984). *Experiential learning: Experience as the source of learning and development*. Englewood Cliffs, NJ; London, UK: Prentice-Hall.

McCabe, C., & Timmins, F. (2013). *Communications skills for nursing practice* (2nd ed.). London, UK: Palgrave Macmillan.

MENCAP. (2016). *Raising our sights guide to communication*. London, UK: MENCAP.

Nursing and Midwifery Council (NMC) (2018). The Code: Professional standards of practice and behaviour for nurses, midwives and nursing associates.

Reid, B. (1993). "But we're doing it already!" Exploring a response to the concept of reflective practice in order to improve its facilitation. *Nurse Education Today*, 13, 305–309..

Rolfe, G., Freshwater, D., & Jasper, M. (2001). *Critical reflection for nursing and the helping professions: A user's guide*. London: Red Globe Press.

Royal College of Nursing. (2017) *Royal College of Nursing employment survey 2017*. London, UK: Royal College of Nursing.

Ruesch, J. (1961). *Therapeutic communication*. New York, NY: Norton.

Schön, D. A. (1983). *The reflective practitioner: How professionals think in action*. New York, NY: Basic Books.

UCL. (2018). *Carotid artery wave intensity measured in mid- to late-life predicts future cognitive decline: The Whitehall II study*. Paper presented at the AHA Scientific Sessions Conference, Chicago, IL, USA.

Veehof, M. M., Oskam, M.-J., Schreurs, K. M. G., & Bohlmeijer, E. T. (2011). Acceptance-based interventions for the treatment of chronic pain: A systematic review and meta-analysis. *PAIN, 152*(3), 533–542.

WHO. (2015). *Obesity – A global problem*. Geneva, Paris: WHO.

World Health Organisation. (2015). *Dementia: A public health priority*. Geneva, Paris: WHO.

Woodhall, L. J., Vertacnik, L., & McLaughlin, M. (2008). Implementation of the SBAR communication technique in a tertiary center. *Journal of Emergency Medicine*, 34, 314–317.

Index

Printed in the USA
CPSIA information can be obtained
at www.ICGtesting.com
LVHW020227030224
770784LV00003B/503